HARRAP'S
ARABIC
pocket
GRAMMAR
AND SCRIPT

D1211313

McGraw Hill

New York Chicago San Francisco Lisbon London Madrid Mexico City
Milan New Delhi San Juan Seoul Singapore Sydney Toronto

ISBN 978-0-07-163617-9
MHID 0-07-163617-X

McGraw-Hill books are available at special quantity discounts to use as
premiums and sales promotions or for use in corporate training programs.
To contact a representative, please visit the Contact Us pages at
www.mhprofessional.com.

Authors: Michael Whitehouse, Aziza Zaher
Consultant: Paul Starkey
Project Editors: Alex Hepworth, Kate Nicholson
With Helen Bleck

Designed by Chambers Harrap Publishers Ltd, Edinburgh
Typeset in Rotis Serif and Meta Plus by Macmillan Publishing Solutions

CONTENTS

INTRODUCTION

This Arabic grammar from Chambers has been written to meet
the needs of all students of Arabic, and is particularly useful for
those taking school examinations. The essential rules of the Arabic
language have been set in terms that are as accessible as possible
to all users. Where technical terms have been used, then full
explanations of these terms have also been supplied. There is also a
glossary of grammatical terminology on pages 7-14.

While literary aspects of the Arabic language have not been
ignored, the emphasis has been placed squarely on Modern
Standard Arabic. This grammar, with its wealth of lively and typical
illustrations of usage taken from the present-day language, is the
ideal study tool for all levels – from the beginner who is starting
to get to grips with the Arabic language through to the advanced
user who requires a comprehensive and readily accessible work of
reference.

This brand-new book boasts a smart colour design to make
consultation even easier and more enjoyable.

Abbreviations used in the text:

acc	accusative
f	feminine
gen	genitive
m	masculine
nom	nominative
pl	plural
sing	singular

GLOSSARY OF GRAMMATICAL TERMS

ACCUSATIVE   The accusative is the case used when a noun or pronoun (and any related adjective) is the object of a verb. For example, in the phrases **I love him** and **I bought a book** the words *him* and *a book* are objects and, in Arabic, must be put in the accusative case. *See* CASE.

ACTIVE   The active form of a verb is the basic form as in **I** *remember* **her**. It is normally opposed to the PASSIVE form of the verb as in **she** *will be remembered*.

ACTIVE PARTICIPLE   The active participle is the person or subject that carries out the action of the verb, eg **translator**, **teacher**. In Arabic, each verb has a set pattern for forming this active participle, eg مُتَرْجِم **translator**, مُدَرِّس **teacher**.

ADJECTIVE   An adjective provides supplementary information about a noun, describing what something is like, eg **a** *small* **house**, **a** *red* **car**, **an** *interesting* **pastime**. In Arabic, adjectives must agree with nouns in number, gender and definiteness.

ADVERB   Adverbs are normally used with a verb to add extra information by indicating how, when, where, with how much intensity or to what extent the action is done. Adverbs may also be used with an adjective or another adverb, eg **a** *very* **attractive girl**, *very* **well**. Arabic does not have a category of words known as adverbs. Instead, adverbs can be formed in a number of different ways.

AGREEMENT In Arabic, words such as adjectives, verbs and pronouns must agree with the noun or pronoun to which they refer. This means that their spelling changes according to the NUMBER of the noun (singular, dual or plural), according to its GENDER (masculine or feminine), according to its definiteness (definite or indefinite) and according to its CASE (nominative, accusative or genitive).

ARTICLE *See* DEFINITE ARTICLE *and* INDEFINITE ARTICLE.

CARDINAL Cardinal numbers are numbers such as **one**, **two**, **ten**, **fourteen**, as opposed to ORDINAL numbers, eg **first**, **second**.

CASE Arabic has three cases (*see* NOMINATIVE, ACCUSATIVE *and* GENITIVE). Each case is indicated by special endings on nouns and adjectives.

CLAUSE A clause is a group of words that contains at least a subject and a verb: **he said** is a clause. A clause often contains more than this basic information, eg **he said this to her yesterday**. Sentences can be made up of several clauses, eg **he said/he'd call me/if he were free**. *See* SENTENCE.

COMPARATIVE The comparative forms of adjectives and adverbs allow two things, people or actions to be compared. In English, **more ... than**; **...er than**; **less ... than** and **as ... as** are used for comparison.

CONDITIONAL This mood is used to describe what someone would do, or something that would happen, if a condition were fulfilled, eg **I** *would come* **if I were well**; **the chair** *would have broken* **if he had sat on it**.

CONJUGATION The conjugation of a verb is the set of different forms taken in the particular tenses of that verb.

CONJUNCTION   Conjunctions are used to link different clauses. They may be coordinating or subordinating. Coordinating conjunctions are words like **and**, **but**, **or**, subordinating conjunctions are words like **because**, **after**, **although**.

DEFINITE ARTICLE   The definite article is **the** in English and ال in Arabic. Proper nouns, such as names, are always definite, although they do not always take the definite article.

DEMONSTRATIVE   Demonstrative adjectives such as **this**, **that**, **these** become PRONOUNS in Arabic, eg هذا and هذه, are used to point out a particular person or object.

DUAL   *See* NUMBER.

EXCLAMATION   An exclamation is a word or sentence used to express surprise or wonder, eg **what!**, **how!**, **how lucky!**, **what a nice day!**

FEMININE   *See* GENDER.

FUTURE   The future tense is used to refer to actions that will happen in the future. In Arabic, there is no future tense as such; instead, the IMPERFECT (present) tense is preceded by س or سوف.

GENDER   The gender of a noun indicates whether the noun is MASCULINE or FEMININE. All Arabic nouns are either masculine or feminine.

GENITIVE   The genitive case is used in Arabic when some form of possession is being expressed, for example as the second part of an IDĀFA construction. The genitive case is also used on nouns that occur after PREPOSITIONS.

IDĀFA The idāfa construction is unique to Arabic. It concerns two or more nouns, where one is the possessor of the other(s), eg باب البيت **the door of the house**, and كتاب الأستاذ **the teacher's book**. An idāfa construction can also be used to translate many compound phrases in English, eg وزارة الداخلية **Interior Ministry**. The last noun of an idāfa is always GENITIVE and can be definite or indefinite. The other nouns of an idāfa must be indefinite, but can take any case.

IMPERATIVE This mood is used for giving orders, eg **eat!**, **don't go!**

IMPERFECT In Arabic the imperfect (or present) tense is used to describe ongoing actions. There are three forms of the imperfect tense: INDICATIVE, JUSSIVE and SUBJUNCTIVE.

INDEFINITE ARTICLE The indefinite article is **a/an** in English. Arabic does not have an indefinite article.

INDICATIVE The imperfect indicative tense is used in Arabic to describe ongoing actions in the present or future, eg **I write, I am writing, I will write**. *See* IMPERFECT.

INFINITIVE The infinitive is the basic form of the verb as found in dictionaries. Thus **to eat** and **to finish** are infinitives. There is no infinitive form of the verb in Arabic; instead, the third person singular form of the past tense is used to list verbs in dictionaries.

INTERROGATIVE Interrogative words are used to ask a question. This may be a direct question (***when** will you arrive?*) or an indirect question (*I don't know **when** he'll arrive*). *See* QUESTION.

JUSSIVE The jussive in Arabic is a form of the imperfect tense, most commonly used after لم to form the negative past tense, eg لم أذهبْ **I did not go**. *See* IMPERFECT.

MASCULINE *See* GENDER.

MOOD This is the name given to the four main areas within which a verb is conjugated. *See* INDICATIVE, SUBJUNCTIVE, CONDITIONAL, IMPERATIVE.

NEGATIVE PARTICLES These are used to make a verb negative. In English, the equivalent of a negative particle is **not**, however Arabic has a wider range, including لن, لم, ما, لا and ليس.

NOMINAL SENTENCE In Arabic, a nominal sentence consists of two parts. It must begin with a noun or pronoun and be followed by a predicate, eg البيت كبير **the house is big**. *See* PREDICATE.

NOMINATIVE The nominative case is the case used when a noun or pronoun (and any related adjective) is the subject of a verb, eg in the phrase **the new caretaker speaks Arabic**, the words *the new caretaker* must be in the nominative case in Arabic.

NOUN A noun is a word or group of words which refers to a living creature, a thing, a place or an abstract idea, eg **postman**, **cat**, **shop**, **passport**, **life**.

NUMBER The number of a noun indicates whether the noun is SINGULAR or PLURAL. A singular noun refers to one single person or thing, eg **boy**, **train** and a plural noun to more than one, eg **boys**, **trains**. Arabic also has DUAL nouns, which are used to refer to two people or things, eg **(two) boys**, **(two) trains**.

OBJECT An object is a noun or a pronoun which follows a verb, eg **I met *a friend***.

OBJECT PRONOUNS Object pronouns in English include **me**, **him**, **her**, **us** etc. In Arabic, these are suffixes added to a verb, eg رأيته **I saw *him*** and يحبها **he loves *her***.

ORDINAL Ordinal numbers are **first**, **second**, **third**, **fourth** and all other numbers which end in **–th** in English.

PASSIVE   A verb is used in the passive when the subject of the verb does not perform the action but is subjected to it. The passive is formed with the verb **to be** and the past participle of the verb, eg **he was rewarded**. It is used in contrast to the **ACTIVE**.

PASSIVE PARTICIPLE   The passive participle describes the person or object upon which the action of the verb was carried out, eg **translated**, **taught**. In Arabic, each verb form has a set pattern for forming this passive participle, eg مُتَرْجَم **translated**, مُدَرَّس **taught**.

PATTERN   Arabic has ten basic verb patterns which all verbs conform to. These are known as أوزان.

PERFECT   In Arabic the perfect (past) tense is used to describe completed actions, eg **I wrote, I have written**.

PERSON   In any tense, there are three persons in the singular (1st: **I**, 2nd: **you**, 3rd: **he/she/it**), and three in the plural (1st: **we**, 2nd: **you**, 3rd: **they**). Arabic also has the 2nd and 3rd person dual, which is used to refer to groups of two people only.

PERSONAL PRONOUNS   Personal pronouns stand for a noun. They can form the first part of a **NOMINAL SENTENCE**, and they can accompany a verb as the verb's subject (**I**, **you**, **he/she/it**, **we**, **they**).

PLURAL   *See* **NUMBER**.

POSSESSIVE   Possessive adjectives and pronouns are used to indicate possession or ownership. They are words like **my/mine**, **your/yours**, **our/ours**.

PREDICATE   The predicate is the part of a clause that refers to the subject, and can be any type of word or phrase, eg in the clause **he is an engineer**, *he* is the subject and the words *is an engineer* make up the predicate.

PREPOSITION   Prepositions are words such as **with**, **in**, **to**, **at**. They are followed by a noun or a pronoun in English. In Arabic, nouns that follow prepositions always take the genitive case. *See* CASE *and* GENITIVE.

PRONOUN   This is a word which stands for a noun. The main categories of pronouns are:
- **Relative pronouns** (eg **who, which, that**)
- **Demonstrative pronouns** (eg **this, that, these**)
- **Possessive pronouns** (eg **mine, yours, his**)
- **Personal pronouns** (eg **you, he, us**)
- **Object pronouns** (eg **me, him, them**)

QUESTION   There are two question forms: direct questions stand on their own and require a question mark at the end, eg **when will he come?**; indirect questions are introduced by a clause and require no question mark, eg **I wonder when he will come**.

ROOT   In Arabic the root of a word usually consists of three consonants that give the word its meaning. Words with the same root tend to be related in meaning and all words are listed under their root in the dictionary. For example, كتاب **book**, كاتب **writer** and مكتبة **bookshop/library** all share the same root: the verb كتب **to write**.

SENTENCE   A sentence is a group of words made up of one or more clauses (*see* CLAUSE) and which makes a complete grammatical structure. The end of a sentence is indicated by a punctuation mark (usually a full stop, a question mark or an exclamation mark).

SINGULAR   *See* NUMBER.

SUBJECT The subject of a verb is the noun or pronoun which performs the action. In the sentences, **the train left early** and **she bought a record**, *the train* and *she* are the subjects. In Arabic, there are two types of subject, one in a verbal sentence, called الفاعل and one in a nominal sentence, called المبتدأ.

SUBJUNCTIVE The subjunctive is a verb form that is rarely used in English, eg **if I were you**, **God save the Queen**. In Arabic, the subjunctive only occurs in the imperfect tense. When two verbs come together, eg **I** *want to go*, the second verb will be a subjunctive. It is also used with negative verbs in the FUTURE tense.

SUFFIX This is an ending which attaches to a word to alter its meaning. In Arabic, the only suffixes are possessive and object pronouns.

SUPERLATIVE The superlative is the form of an adjective or an adverb which, in English, is marked by **the most ...**, **the ...est** or **the least ...**.

TENSE Verbs are used in tenses, which tell us whether an action takes place in the present, the past or the future. There are two main tenses in Arabic, the perfect (or past) tense and the imperfect (or present) tense. *See* IMPERFECT *and* PERFECT.

VERB A verb is a word that describes the performance of an action, eg **to sing**, **to work**, **to watch** or the existence of a state, eg **to be**, **to have**, **to hope**. In Arabic, the verb **to be** is not generally used.

VERBAL NOUN A verbal noun in English is formed by adding the suffix **-ing** to a verb, eg **walking**. In Arabic, verbal nouns can be used to form adverbs. *See* ADVERB.

VERBAL SENTENCE A verbal sentence in Arabic begins with a verb, which is followed by the subject.

1 THE ALPHABET

Arabic is written from right to left. The Arabic alphabet has 28 letters (29 if **hamza** (ء) is counted as a letter in its own right), and is made up of consonants, three of which function as long vowels. There are also a number of additional signs and symbols. Short vowels are generally not written, except in formal texts.

A. THE LETTERS, TRANSLITERATION AND PRONUNCIATION

Letter	Name	Transliteration	Pronunciation
ا	`alif	a/ā	cab/car/care
ب	bā`	b	**b**ar
ت	tā`	t	**t**en
ث	thā`	th	**th**in
ج	jīm	j	**j**oke
ح	ḥā`	ḥ	**
خ	khā`	kh	Ba**ch**/lo**ch**
د	dāl	d	**d**og
ذ	dhāl	dh	**th**at
ر	rā`	r	rolled **r**
ز	zāy	z	**z**igzag
س	sīn	s	**s**it
ش	shīn	sh	**sh**ut
ص	ṣād	ṣ	**
ض	ḍād	ḍ	**
ط	ṭā`	ṭ	**
ظ	ḍhā`	ḍh	**
ع	`ayn	`	**

غ	ghayn	gh	**
ف	fāʾ	f	**f**oot
ق	qāf	q	**
ك	kāf	k	**k**ettle
ل	lām	l	**l**eg
م	mīm	m	**m**osque
ن	nūn	n	**n**ever
ه	hāʾ	h	**h**at
و	wāw	w/ū	**w**et/l**oo**t
ي	yāʾ	y/ī	**y**es/f**ee**t
ء	hamza	ʾ	*See* Section D

** There are no equivalent sounds in English for these letters. The following should act as a guide to their pronunciation:

Letter	Name	Pronunciation
ح	ḥāʾ	a very breathy *h*
ع	ʿayn	an *ah* sound from the very back of the throat
غ	ghayn	similar to a rolled French *r* as in 'Paris', or the sound produced when gargling
ق	qāf	a *k* from the very back of the throat

The following four letters are emphatic sounds, which are spoken with the tongue placed halfway back along the roof of the mouth:

Letter	Name	Pronunciation
ص	ṣād	**s**ob
ض	ḍād	**d**ot
ط	ṭāʾ	**t**op
ظ	dhā	**th**ough

B. JOINING THE LETTERS

Unlike English, Arabic has no capital letters. However, there are four different ways of writing most letters, depending on whether they appear at the beginning of a word (initial), in the middle (medial), at the end (final) or on their own (isolated). Arabic is a cursive script, meaning that most of the letters are joined.

All letters can be joined to a preceding letter, and all but six can be joined to the following letter. The table below shows the Arabic letters in their four forms:

Name	Final	Medial	Initial	Isolated	Examples
`alif	ـا	ـا	ا	ا*	اسم ، فاعل ، سوريا
bā`	ـب	ـبـ	بـ	ب	باب ، كبير ، بسبب
tā`	ـت	ـتـ	تـ	ت	تجارة ، أنتم ، أنت
thā`	ـث	ـثـ	ثـ	ث	ثلاث ، اثنان ، حيث
jīm	ـج	ـجـ	جـ	ج	جميل ، دجاج ، حج
ḥā`	ـح	ـحـ	حـ	ح	حديقة ، صحيح ، صباح
khā`	ـخ	ـخـ	خـ	خ	أخبار ، الخرطوم ، شيخ
dāl	ـد	ـد	د	د*	دب ، جديد ، ولد
dhāl	ـذ	ـذ	ذ	ذ*	ذلك ، مذاكرة ، لذيذ
rā`	ـر	ـر	ر	ر*	راديو ، مريض ، جسر
zāy	ـز	ـز	ز	ز*	زيارة ، عزيز ، وزير
sīn	ـس	ـسـ	سـ	س	سلام ، السودان ، مدرّس
shīn	ـش	ـشـ	شـ	ش	شديد ، مشمس ، درويش
ṣād	ـص	ـصـ	صـ	ص	صباح ، مصر ، نصوص
ḍād	ـض	ـضـ	ضـ	ض	ضابط ، بيضاء ، أبيض
ṭā`	ـط	ـطـ	طـ	ط	طماطم ، بطاطس ، محيط

dhā`	ظ–	ظ–	ظ	ظ	ظهر ، مظاهرة ، حظ
`ayn	ع	ﻌ	ﻋ	ع	عربي ، بعد ، بيع ، جوع
ghayn	غ	ﻐ	ﻏ	غ	غبي ، المغرب ، دماغ
fā`	ف–	ﻔ–	ﻓ	ف	فيلم ، مفتاح ، خريف
qāf	ق–	ﻘ–	ﻗ	ق	قديم ، دقيقة ، دمشق
kāf	ك–	ﻜ–	ﻛ	ك	كلمة ، الكويت ، ملك
lām	ل–	ﻠ–	ﻟ	ل	لسان ، مليون ، جبل ، جبال
mīm	م–	ﻤ–	ﻣ	م	مدرسة ، اسماء ، نعم
nūn	ن–	ﻨ–	ﻧ	ن	نوع ، بنت ، بين ، إنسان
hā`	ﻪ	ﻬ	ﻫ	ه	هذا ، نهر ، وجه ، دكتوراه
wāw	و–	و–	و	*و	ولاية ، أسبوع ، حلو
yā`	ي	ﻴ–	ﻳ	ي	يونان ، كبير ، التي ، شاي

* These are the six letters that do not join to any following letters.

> **Note**
> When the letter ل (**lām**) occurs before ا (`**alif**), they are written together as لا and do not join to following letters. When preceded by another **lām**, لا becomes للا. For example:
>
> للإنسان **lil-insān**   لائم **lā`im**   سلام **salām**

C. VOWELS

Arabic has three long vowels and three short vowels. The three long vowels ا (`**alif**), و (**wāw**) and ي (**yā`**) are shown in the 28 letters of the alphabet in **Section A**.

The short vowels appear above or below the consonant they follow, but are not often written and are not considered part of the 28 letters of the alphabet. They are used in dictionaries, texts for children and the Qur'an, but are rarely given elsewhere and almost never appear in handwriting. The short vowels are as follows:

Vowel	Name	Pronunciation
َ	fat<u>h</u>a	c**a**t
ُ	<u>d</u>amma	p**u**t
ِ	kasra	s**i**t
ْ	sukūn	used when no vowel follows the consonant

For example:

وَلَد **walad**   دراسة **dirāsah**

فُطور **futūr**   بِنت **bint**

Arabic also has two diphthongs, formed by combining the short vowel **fat<u>h</u>a** with the long vowels و (**wāw**) and ي (**yā`**):

Diphthong	Transliteration	Pronunciation	Examples
وَ	aw	d**ow**n	مَوْت **mawt** (not mūt)
يَ	ay	b**ai**t	بَيْت **bayt** (not bīt)

D. SPECIAL LETTERS AND SYMBOLS

1 Tā` marbū<u>t</u>a

Tā` marbū<u>t</u>a is used at the end of a word, its main function being to make a noun or adjective feminine. It can appear as ة if it is not joined to its preceding letter or as ـة if it is joined.

Tā` marbū<u>t</u>a is pronounced as an *a* or *ah* sound, unless the word forms part of an **idāfa** construction, in which case it is pronounced as *at*:

مدينة **madīnah**

مدينة السلام **madīnat as-salām**

2 Shadda

A **shadda** (ّ) doubles a letter:

دَرَّسَ **dar̲rasa**

3 `Alif maqsūra

This letter (ى) appears at the end of certain words, and is
pronounced as a long *a* sound:

المَقهَى **al-maqhā**

4 `Alif mādda/`Alif mamdūda

When two `**alifs** occur together, they become `**alif mādda** (آ), also
known as `**alif mamdūda**. This is pronounced as a **hamza** followed
by a long *a* sound:

أ + ا = آ

آسِف **āsif**

5 Hamza (hamzat al-qat̲)

A **hamza** is often referred to as a glottal stop, and is similar to
the sound produced when saying the English word 'letter' and
dropping the *t* sound (le'er).

On its own, a **hamza** is written ء and is usually transliterated
using an apostrophe. However, a **hamza** can appear in many
different forms. The rules governing **hamza** are complicated, and
are based on a hierarchy of the short vowels. The 'strongest'
vowel is **kasra**, followed by **d̲amma** and then **fath̲a**. **Sukūn** is the
weakest vowel.

a) A **hamza** at the start of a word is always written with an `**alif**
and one of the short vowels:

أ with **fath̲a** (*a*)

أ with **d̲amma** (*u*)

إ with **kasra** (*i*)

b) When a **hamza** appears in the middle of a word, it is necessary to examine the short vowels either side of it. The stronger of the two vowels dictates how the **hamza** is written:

- If **kasra** is the stronger, the **hamza** is written on a 'seat': ئ

- If **damma** is the stronger, the **hamza** is written above a **wāw**: ؤ

- If **fatha** is the stronger, the **hamza** is written above an `alif: أ

- If the **hamza** comes after an `alif or a **wāw**, and the following vowel is a **fatha**, the **hamza** is written on the line: ء

- If the **hamza** comes after a **yā**` or the diphthong **ay**, the **hamza** is written on a 'seat': ئ

c) When a **hamza** appears at the end of a word, the vowel before the **hamza** dictates how it is written:

- If **kasra** comes before the **hamza**, the **hamza** is written ئ

- If **damma** comes before the **hamza**, it is written ؤ

- If **fatha** comes before the **hamza**, it is written أ

- If **sukūn** comes before the **hamza**, it is written ء

6 Hamzat al-waṣl

The definite article in Arabic is ال. Instead of carrying a **hamza**, the definite article carries a **hamzat al-waṣl** (ٱ), which does not affect the pronunciation, and generally is not written except in very formal texts. **Hamzat al-waṣl** also occurs with certain verb forms, such as استفعل, and a few nouns, for example اسم and امرأة.

7 Tanwīn al-fath

Because short vowels are not written in most texts, case endings (which appear as short vowels on the ends of words) do not normally appear in written Arabic. However, one case ending, known as **tanwīn al-fath**, affects the spelling of the word itself. This is used with a number of adverbs and to mark indefinite

nouns in the accusative case. It appears with an `alif as اً, which
is pronounced *an*:

شكراً **shukran**   بيتاً **baytan**

Tanwīn al-fath is not written with an `alif in nouns ending in
ة, ء or ى. Instead, it appears as two lines above these letters: ةً,
ءً and ىً. These lines are not written in most texts, but are still
pronounced as *an*.

عادةً ' **ādatan**   مقهىً **maqhan**

See also **Chapter 4, Section B** *and* **Chapter 6.**

E. ARABIC NUMERALS

Arabic numerals are written as follows:

0	·	5	٥
1	١	6	٦
2	٢	7	٧
3	٣	8	٨
4	٤	9	٩

Some Arabic-speaking countries, especially those in North Africa,
do not use the Arabic numbers and instead use the same system as
European languages.

In contrast to the Arabic alphabet, numbers made up of more than
one digit are written from left to right.

١٥	٥·١	٧٣	٢··٩
15	501	73	2009

Decimals are written using commas instead of full stops:

٤,٥	٣,٧٥
4.5	3.75

Dates are written in the same direction as Arabic script, from right to left:

٢٠٠٩/١٢/٢٥
25/12/2009

See Chapter 16 *for more on numerals.*

2 THE ROOT SYSTEM

In Arabic almost all words can be traced to an identifiable root (جذر). Words that share a common root are often related in meaning, as may be seen from the following, which are all derived from the root ك / ت / ب:

مكتوب	كاتب	كتب
written	writer	wrote

مكتب	كتاب	كتابة
office	book	writing

		مكتبة
		library

The root of a word gives its basic meaning and is usually made up of three (occasionally four) consonants. These letters can be used to form other words (derivatives) according to certain common patterns. For example, to make a noun that refers to the agent of an action, we can use the pattern for three-letter verbs, known as فاعِل, inserting an ا after the first root letter.

كاتب	→	كتب
writer		wrote

دارس	→	درس
student		studied

عالم	→	علم
scientist		knew

فاتح	→	فتح
opener		opened

Some roots are made up of four letters, for example:

ترجم	دحرج	زلزل
translate	roll	earthquake

Knowledge of the root and patterns system is the key to improving your vocabulary. It is also important to be able to identify the root of a word in order to use an Arabic dictionary, where words are listed according to their roots, rather than their full forms. For example, to look up the word مستقبل (future), the three-letter root must be identified as ق / ب / ل. The word will be listed in most dictionaries under this root.

All words that have the same root are listed together and it is necessary to identify the correct word from the list. However, most dictionaries do not list those words that are regular in pattern, such as دارس (student) and مدروس (studied), so it is extremely important to have some knowledge of verb forms and the root system.

It is also important to bear in mind that `alif (١) itself never functions as a root letter. Words that appear to have `alif (١) as one of their root letters are likely in fact to be based on a root containing either و or ي. This point is particularly important in connection with weak and hollow verbs (*see* **Chapter 13, Section I**).

3 THE DEFINITE ARTICLE

In Arabic, definite nouns and adjectives are marked by the definite article ('the' in English), while indefinite nouns and adjectives remain unmarked.

A. FORM OF THE DEFINITE ARTICLE

The definite article is formed by the prefix ال which is written at the beginning of the word and is joined to it. In written Arabic, the definite article is the same whether the noun is singular, dual or plural, feminine or masculine, for example:

رجل	الرجل
a man	the man
رجال	الرجال
men	the men
بنت	البنت
a girl	the girl
بنات	البنات
girls	the girls

The pronunciation of the definite article (ال) depends on the first sound of the word it joins. The 28 Arabic letters are classified into two groups according to the way they affect the pronunciation of the definite article.

1   The sun letters

The sun letters are the 14 letters in Arabic with which the definite article ال loses its distinctive sound, and is instead pronounced in the same way as the first sound of the word. As a result, the first sound of the word is doubled. This can be indicated by a **shadda** (´) on the first letter of the word.

English	Transliteration	Arabic	Sun letter
the merchant	at-tājir	التّاجر	ت
the ice	ath-thalj	الثّلج	ث
the bear	ad-dubb	الدّب	د
the corn	adh-dhura	الذّرة	ذ
the spring	ar-rabī'	الرّبيع	ر
the giraffe	az-zarāfa	الزّرافة	ز
the sky	as-samā'	السّماء	س
the sun	ash-shams	الشّمس	ش
the morning	aṣ-ṣabāḥ	الصّباح	ص
the fog	aḍ-ḍabāb	الضّباب	ض
the student	aṭ-ṭālib	الطّالب	ط
the darkness	adh-dhalām	الظلام	ظ
the light	an-nūr	النّور	ن
the night	al-layl	الليل	ل

2 The moon letters

The moon letters are the 14 Arabic letters which do not affect the sound of the definite article (ال) at the beginning of the word.

English	Transliteration	Arabic	Moon letter
the brother	al-'akh	الأخ	أ
the door	al-bāb	الباب	ب
the camel	al-jamal	الجمل	ج
the horse	al-ḥiṣān	الحصان	ح
the sheep	al-kharūf	الخروف	خ
the eye	al-'ayn	العين	ع
the crow	al-ghurāb	الغراب	غ
the knight	al-fāris	الفارس	ف
the moon	al-qamar	القمر	ق
the speech	al-kalām	الكلام	ك

the manager	**al-mudīr**	المدير	م
the air	**al-hawā'**	الهواء	هـ
the father	**al-wālid**	الوالد	و
the hand	**al-yad**	اليد	ي

B. FUNCTIONS OF THE DEFINITE ARTICLE

In Arabic, the definite article is generally used in the following instances:

1 With nouns that refer to objects known to the speaker for three main reasons

a) The noun has been mentioned before in the text, for example:

أعطيت صديقتي هدية، فقبلت الهدية

I gave my friend a present, so she accepted **the present**

b) The noun refers to something that is common knowledge to all speakers, for example:

البيت الجديد واسع ومريح

the new house is spacious and comfortable

c) The noun refers to something or someone present at the time of speaking, for example:

أخيراً وصل القطار!

at last, **the train** has arrived!

2 With abstract nouns that refer to a general idea or concept

الحرية والديموقراطية مطلب كل الشعوب

freedom and **democracy** are demanded by all people

السلام والعدالة أساس الرخاء

peace and **justice** are the basis of prosperity

3 With nouns that refer to all members of, or items in, a certain group

المرأة تساوي الرجل

women are equal to **men**

العرب مشهورون بالكرم وحسن الضيافة

the Arabs are known for generosity and hospitality

4 With certain geographical names (country names, cities, seas, mountains, etc)

أتمنى أن أسافر إلى الهند والصين

I hope to travel to **India** and **China**

صديقتي فاطمة تسكن في مدينة الرباط في المغرب

my friend Fatima lives in **the city of Rabat** in **Morocco**

المحيط الهادي هو أكبر محيطات العالم

the Pacific Ocean is the largest ocean in the world

Note that all ocean names take the definite article in Arabic. The following is a list of country names that begin with the definite article:

Argentina	الأرجنتين
Jordan	الأردن
Emirates	الإمارات
Bahrain	البحرين
Brazil	البرازيل
Portugal	البرتغال
Bosnia and Herzegovina	البوسنة والهرسك
Algeria	الجزائر
Congo	الكونغو
Denmark	الدانمرك
El Salvador	السلفادور
Senegal	السنغال

Sudan	السودان
Sweden	السويد
Somalia	الصومال
China	الصين
Iraq	العراق
Philippines	الفلبين
Cameroon	الكاميرون
Kuwait	الكويت
Hungary	المجر
Morocco	المغرب
Mexico	المكسيك
Saudi Arabia	السعودية
Norway	النرويج
Austria	النمسا
Niger	النيجر
India	الهند
Japan	اليابان
Yemen	اليمن
Greece	اليونان

5 With specific titles or job titles

محمد علي باشا – الوالي العثماني – هو مؤسس مصر الحديثة

Mohammed Ali Pasha – **the Ottoman ruler** – is the founder of modern Egypt

الرئيس الأمريكي يقابل الملك السعودي في الرياض

the American President meets **the Saudi King** in Riyadh

6 With names and acronyms of certain organizations

الأمم المتحدة تهدف لتحقيق السلام في العالم

the UN aims to achieve world peace

الأوبك تحدد أسعار النفط العالمية
OPEC defines the world price of oil

7 With the names of important historical events

الثورة الصناعية غيّرت أوروبا
the Industrial revolution changed Europe

الحرب العالمية الثانية أثرت في الشرق الأوسط
the Second World War affected the Middle East region

8 With languages

أدرس العربية والفرنسية والإسبانية في الجامعة
I study **Arabic, French** and **Spanish** at university

9 With the days of the week

الأربعاء موعد زيارة صديقتي والخميس موعد زيارة الطبيب
Wednesday is the day I visit my friend, and **Thursday** is my doctor's
appointment

10 With the seasons of the year

في الربيع والخريف درجة الحرارة معتدلة
in **spring** and **autumn**, the temperature is mild

11 With names of religions, sects and holy books, as well as names of political and ideological movements

الإسلام والمسيحية أكثر الديانات انتشاراً في مصر
Islam and **Christianity** are the most widespread religions in Egypt

القرآن هو الكتاب المقدس للمسلمين
the Qur'an is the holy book for Muslims

الرأسمالية منتشرة في البلدان الغربية
capitalism is widespread in Western countries

4 NOUNS

Nouns are words used to refer to people or things and can be definite or indefinite, feminine or masculine, singular, dual or plural:

المفكّر	المفكّرون
the thinker	the thinkers
شجرة	الأشجار
a tree	the trees
فكرة	أفكار
an idea	ideas
طالب	محمد
a student	Mohammed

A. DEFINITE NOUNS

There are several types of definite noun in Arabic: proper nouns, nouns ending with a possessive pronoun and nouns forming the first term in an **idāfa** (genitive) construction (*see* **Section E**), among others. However, the definite article ال is the most common marker of definite nouns. *For more information on the definite article see* **Chapter 3**.

B. INDEFINITE NOUNS

Arabic does not use indefinite articles ('a' or 'an' in English). However, in formal Arabic most indefinite nouns and adjectives are marked by the addition of a *n* sound to the short final vowel at the end of the word. This *n* sound, known as **tanwīn**, is not written as a full consonant but is marked by a doubling of the vowel sign: ´ becomes ˝, ˛ becomes ˛, and ˌ becomes ˌ.

هو طالبٌ

he is a student

قابلت طالباً فرنسياً في الجامعة

I met a French student at the university

The following examples show some typical uses of indefinite nouns.

1 As an indefinite object

شاهدت رجلاً كبيراً في الشارع

I saw **an old man** in the street

اشتريت هديةً لزوجتي

I bought **a present** for my wife

2 To describe another noun as a predicate of a nominal sentence

أنا مدرسةٌ وأخي مهندسٌ

I am **a teacher**, and my brother is **an engineer**

مراد أستاذٌ في جامعة القاهرة

Murad is **a professor** at Cairo University

Note that a definite noun may also appear in this position.

3 After the expressions هناك and يوجد (there is/are)

هناك مشكلاتٌ اقتصاديةٌ كثيرة في دول شمال أفريقيا

there are **many economic problems** in North African countries

يوجد مدخلٌ واحدٌ لهذا المبنى

there is **only one entrance** to this building

4 After the question word كم (how many) and after numbers

كم طالباً في الصف؟

how many **students** are there in the class?

في الصف عشرون طالباً

there are twenty **students**

5 In questions and answers about possessions

هل عندك سيارةٌ؟

do you have **a car**?

نعم، عندي سيارةٌ

yes, I have **a car**

لا، ليست عندي سيارةٌ

no, I don't have **a car**

C. GENDER

In Arabic, all nouns are either feminine or masculine.

1 Human nouns

Nouns that refer to humans usually have both a feminine and a masculine form, corresponding to the physical gender of the person:

رجل	امرأة
man	woman
رجال	نساء
men	women
طالب	طالبة
student *(m)*	student *(f)*
مدير	مديرة
manager *(m)*	manager *(f)*

Masculine nouns are usually unmarked, while feminine nouns are marked by certain suffixes. **Tā` marbūta** (ة) is the most important feminine suffix. It can be added to most masculine nouns to make them feminine. For example:

موظف	موظفة
employee *(m)*	employee *(f)*
مدرّس	مدرّسة
teacher *(m)*	teacher *(f)*

تلميذة	تلميذ
pupil *(f)*	pupil *(m)*

Other feminine suffixes, such as ى and اء, are often used to mark proper nouns, particularly names. For example:

منى	وفاء
Mona	Wafaa'
ليلى	أسماء
Laila	Asmaa'
لبنى	هناء
Lobna	Hana'
هدى	علياء
Huda	Alya'

It should be noted that some masculine proper nouns can also end in what appear to be feminine suffixes, for example حمزة (Hamza) among others.

2 Non-human nouns

Nouns that do not refer to human beings also have gender. Inanimate nouns can be either masculine or feminine, and the relationship between the noun and gender is arbitrary. Most, but not all feminine non-human nouns can be identified because they end in **tā` marbūta** (ة):

باب	نافذة
door *(m)*	window *(f)*
كرسي	طاولة
chair *(m)*	table *(f)*
قمر	شمس
moon *(m)*	sun *(f)*
بحر	بحيرة
sea *(m)*	lake *(f)*

الكرسي أبيض والطاولة بنية
the chair is white, and the table is brown

البحر كبير والبحيرة صغيرة
the sea is large, and the lake is small

D. NUMBER

In Arabic, nouns can be singular, dual, or plural. Singular nouns are not marked for number, but dual and plural nouns are marked.

Dual nouns are marked by suffixes. Plural nouns can be sound (regular) or broken (irregular). Sound plurals are marked by suffixes alone, while broken plurals are marked by internal changes in word form.

1 Dual

Dual nouns are used to refer to two things or people, for example كتابان (two books). Dual nouns are marked by the suffix ان in the nominative and by the suffix ـيْن in the accusative or genitive case:

كتاب	كتابان / كتابين
book	two books
رجل	رجلان / رجلين
man	two men
طالب	طالبان / طالبين
student *(m)*	two students *(m)*

If the noun ends with **tā` marbūta** (ة), then ة becomes ت when the dual suffix is added to the word:

قصة	قصتان / قصتين
story	two stories
امرأة	امرأتان / امرأتين
woman	two women

طالبة student *(f)*	طالبتان / طالبتين two students *(f)*

The dual is used whenever two objects or people are referred to, but *never* for more than two objects or people:

مايسة وهناء طالبتان في جامعتين مختلفتين
Maysa and Hana' are students in two different universities

محمد ومصطفى صديقان
Mohammed and Mustafa are friends

قرأت كتابين وقصتين
I read two books and two stories

لي صديقتان
I have two friends

The dual noun must be masculine when it refers to two masculine nouns, or to one masculine and one feminine noun. The dual noun must be feminine only when *both* nouns referred to are feminine people or things:

محمد ومصطفى طالبان
Mohammed and Mustafa are students *(m)*

منى ومحمد طالبان
Mona and Mohammed are students *(m)*

منى وسامية طالبتان
Mona and Samia are students *(f)*

2 Plural

The plural is used to refer to three or more things or people. There are two main types of plural in Arabic: sound (regular) and broken (irregular). Sound plurals are formed by adding suffixes to the end of a word. Broken plurals, on the other hand, change the form of the word.

a) Sound (regular) plurals

There are two types of sound plurals, masculine and feminine. With very few exceptions, the masculine sound plural is used with masculine human nouns only. The suffix ون is added to the noun in the nominative case, ie when the noun is in the subject position. The suffix ين is added to the noun in the accusative case, ie when it is in the object position, or genitive case, ie in **idāfa** constructions or after prepositions.

موظف	موظفون / موظفين
employee (m)	employees (m)
مهندس	مهندسون / مهندسين
engineer (m)	engineers (m)
مدرّس	مدرّسون / مدرّسين
teacher (m)	teachers (m)

محمد ومصطفى وعلى مهندسون في شركة كبيرة
Mohammed, Mustafa and Ali are engineers in a big company

قابلت المهندسين المصريين
I met the Egyptian engineers

The sound feminine plural is formed by replacing the feminine suffix ة with the suffix ات at the end of a feminine noun, or by adding ات to the word itself. It can be used with both human and non-human nouns:

موظفة	موظفات
employee (f)	employees (f)
مهندسة	مهندسات
engineer (f)	engineers (f)
جامعة	جامعات
university	universities

ليلى وجميلة وعلية مهندسات في شركة كبيرة
Laila, Jameela and 'Aleya are engineers in a big company

قابلت المهندسات المصريات
I met the Egyptian engineers *(f)*

b) Broken (irregular) plurals

Broken plurals are formed by changing the pattern of vowels
within words, thus altering their shape. They can be formed with
human or non-human nouns, whether masculine or feminine.
Although most feminine human nouns have sound plural forms,
some take broken plurals.

ولد	أولاد
boy	boys
درس	دروس
lesson	lessons
أسرة	أسر
family	families
حقيبة	حقائب
bag	bags

Broken plurals fall into a number of patterns, some more
common than others. However, there are no rules to specify
which patterns are used with which nouns, so you will need to
keep checking in a dictionary until patterns begin to emerge.
Some of the more common patterns of broken plurals are listed
below:

Singular		Plural	Singular		Plural
	فَعَلَة			فُعَل	
طالب	طَلَبَة	student	أُسْرة	أُسَرٌ	family
حامل	→ حَمَلَة	holder	غُرْفة	→ غُرَفٌ	room
قاتِل	قَتَلَة	killer	جُمْلة	جُمَلٌ	sentence

NOUNS

فُعُل

مَدينة	مُدُنٌ	city
كِتاب →	كُتُبٌ	book
رَسول	رُسُلٌ	messenger

فُعَلاءُ

ناشط	نُشَطاءُ	activist
حَكيم →	حُكَماءُ	wise
غَريب	غُرَباءُ	stranger

فِعَلٌ

قِطْعة	قِطَعٌ	piece
إِبْرة →	إِبَرٌ	needle
مِهْنة	مِهَنٌ	profession

أَفْعِلَةٌ

سُؤال	أَسْئِلةٌ	question
جَواب →	أَجْوِبةٌ	answer
دَيْر	أَدْيِرةٌ	monastery

فُعُولٌ

دَرْس	دُروسٌ	lesson
فَصْل →	فُصولٌ	season
بَيْت	بُيوتٌ	house

أَفْعِلاءُ

قَريب	أَقْرِباءُ	relative
بَريئ →	أَبْرِياءُ	innocent
شَقِي	أَشْقِياءُ	miserable

فِعَالٌ

بَلَد	بِلادٌ	country
جَمَل →	جِمالٌ	camel
خَروف	خِرافٌ	sheep

فُعْلانٌ

بَلَد	بُلْدانٌ	country
راهب →	رُهْبانٌ	monk
حَمَل	حُمْلانٌ	lamb

فُعَّالٌ

عامِل	عُمَّالٌ	worker
كاتب →	كُتَّابٌ	writer
قارِئ	قُرّاءُ	reader

فَعْلَى

جَوْعان	جَوْعَى	hungry
مَريض →	مَرْضَى	ill
عَطْشان	عَطْشَى	thirsty

	فَوَاعِلُ				أَفْعُل	
عامِل	عَوامِلُ	factor		لِسان	أَلْسُنُ	tongue
شارِع	شَوارِعُ	street	→	شَهْر	أَشْهُرُ	month
قالِب	قَوالِبُ	mould		رِجل	أَرْجُلٌ	foot

	مَفاعِلُ				فَعائِلُ	
مَصنَع	مَصانِعُ	factory		عَروس	عَرائِسُ	bride
مَدْرَسة	مَدارِسُ	school	→	قَبيلة	قَبائِلُ	tribe
مَكتَب	مكاتبُ	office		رِسالة	رَسائِلُ	message

	أَفاعيلُ				أَفاعِل	
إقْليم	أَقاليمُ	province		أَرْمَل	أَرامِلُ	widow
أُسْلُوب	أَساليبُ	style	→	مَكان	أَماكِنُ	place
أُسْبُوع	أَسابيعُ	week		قَريب	أَقارِبُ	relative

c) Agreement of plural nouns

Any word that occurs together with a plural noun (verb, adjective, pronoun *etc*) must agree with the noun. However, the agreement between these types of words and the noun depends to a large extent on whether the noun is human or non-human.

i) Any word that occurs with a plural *human noun* must agree with it both in gender and in number:

هم مهندسون مصريون يعملون في لبنان
they are Egyptian engineers working in Lebanon *(m pl)*

هن مهندسات مصريات يعملن في لبنان
they are Egyptian engineers working in Lebanon *(f pl)*

ii) Plural *non-human nouns* are treated as feminine singular nouns and any word that occurs with a plural non-human noun must therefore be feminine singular:

السيارات الجديدة تعمل بالطاقة الشمسية

new cars work with solar power

الكتب الجديدة تتكلم عن موضوعات جيدة

the new books discuss good subjects

E. IDĀFA CONSTRUCTION

The **idāfa** construction (genitive case) can usually be translated as 'of' or with the possessive marker (eg 'Mary**'s** cat') in English. In Arabic a genitive (or **idāfa**) construction is typically made up of two nouns, or a noun and a pronoun. The first noun in a genitive construction must be indefinite in form. However, it remains definite in meaning, as its meaning becomes related to the following noun. The second noun is usually definite, but can be indefinite in some cases.

كتاب الأدب	قلم الطالب
literature book	the student's pen
أساتذة الجامعة	دفاتر الأولاد
university professors	the children's copybooks
غرفة نوم	فنجان قهوة
bedroom	a cup of coffee

Sometimes a genitive construction is composed of a noun and a possessive pronoun, for example:

كتابي	قلمه
my book	his pen
أساتذتنا	دفاترهم
our professors	their copybooks

If the first noun of the genitive construction is a dual or sound

masculine plural, ie it ends in one of the suffixes ‫ان‬, ‫يْن‬ or ‫ون‬, ‫ين‬,
then the final ‫ن‬ is removed:

‫مهندسو الشركة‬	‫والدا البنت‬
company engineers	the girl's parents
‫معلمو المدرسة‬	‫قدما الطفل‬
school teachers	the baby's feet

The same applies if the genitive construction is composed of a noun
and a possessive pronoun:

‫مهندسوها‬	‫والداي‬
its engineers	my parents

5 ADJECTIVES

Adjectives are words used to describe nouns. Just like nouns, they can be definite or indefinite, feminine or masculine, singular, dual or plural, for example:

جديدة	جديد
new	new
الجديدة	الجديد
new	new
كبيرتان	كبيران
big	big
مصريات	مصريون
Egyptian	Egyptian

A. POSITION OF ADJECTIVES

Unlike English, adjectives in Arabic follow the nouns they describe, for example:

طالبة جديدة	طالب جديد
a new student (f)	a new student (m)

B. AGREEMENT

Adjectives agree with the nouns they describe in number, gender and definiteness:

امرأة عربية	رجل عربي
Arab woman	Arab man
نساء عربيات	رجال عرب
Arab women	Arab men

المرأة العربية
the Arab woman

الرجل العربي
the Arab man

1 Gender agreement

Just like nouns, masculine adjectives are usually unmarked, while feminine adjectives are marked with certain suffixes, such as **tā` marbūṭa** (ة), ى or اء. Adjectives and nouns must agree with each other in gender, for example:

موظفة كبيرة
an important employee *(f)*

موظف كبير
an important employee *(m)*

بنت طويلة
a tall girl

ولد طويل
a tall boy

كراسة صفراء
a yellow copybook

كتاب أصفر
a yellow book

آسيا الصغرى
Asia Minor

الشرق الأوسط
the Middle East

There are very few exceptions to this rule, one example being that the adjective for 'pregnant' (حامل) is always in the masculine form although it is used with feminine nouns.

2 Number agreement

a) Formation of singular adjectives

Just like nouns, singular adjectives are unmarked – there are no suffixes or other markers to show their number. For example:

سعيدة
happy *(f)*

سعيد
happy

صغيرة
small *(f)*

عطشان
thirsty

b) Formation of dual adjectives

In the same way as dual nouns, dual adjectives are marked by the suffix ان in the nominative case, or by the suffix ـيْن in the accusative or genitive case.

If the adjective ends with **tā` marbūta** (ة), then it becomes ت when the dual suffix is added to the word. Adjectives agree with nouns in case as well as number, and so they must take the same form of suffix as the noun:

كتابين كبيرين	كتابان كبيران
two big books *(acc/gen)*	two big books *(nom)*
قصتين قصيرتين	قصتان قصيرتان
two short stories *(acc/gen)*	two short stories *(nom)*
امرأتين كبيرتين	رجلان كبيران
two old women *(acc/gen)*	two old men *(nom)*
طالبين مجتهدين	طالبتان عربيتان
two hardworking students *(acc/gen)*	two Arab students *(nom)*

c) Formation of plural adjectives
Plural human nouns must be followed by adjectives that agree with them in number and gender. Just like nouns, some adjectives have sound plurals, while others have broken plurals (*see* **Chapter 4, Section D**).

Plural feminine adjectives are marked with the suffix ات instead of ة. Plural masculine adjectives can either be sound, ie ending with the suffix ون or ـين, or broken.

موظفات لبنانيات	موظفون لبنانيون
Lebanese employees *(f)*	Lebanese employees *(m)*
نساء لبنانيات	موظفين لبنانيين
Lebanese women	Lebanese men
مهندسات عربيات	مهندسون عرب
Arab engineers *(f)*	Arab engineers *(m)*

ليلى وجميلة وعلية مهندسات جديدات في شركة كبيرة
Laila, Jameela and 'Aleya are new engineers in a big company

هم مهندسون جدد يعملون مع مهندسين كويتيين

they are new engineers, working with Kuwaiti engineers

Adjectives that follow non-human plurals are always feminine singular:

الشركات الكبيرة

the big companies

جامعات أمريكية

American universities

البيوت الواسعة

the spacious houses

أحصنة عربية

Arabian horses

الدول العربية

the Arab countries

معابد قديمة

Ancient temples

C. COMPARATIVE AND SUPERLATIVE ADJECTIVES

Comparative adjectives are formed by taking the three-letter root of an adjective and adding أ to the beginning, to give the form known as أفعل. There is no separate feminine form. For example:

غني → أغنى

rich → richer

سعيد → أسعد

happy → happier

صغيرة → أصغر

small → smaller

رخيص → أرخص

cheap → cheaper

'Than' in comparative constructions is expressed by the preposition من, for example:

البنت أصغر من أخيها

the girl is younger than her brother

الفضة أرخص من الذهب

silver is cheaper than gold

The superlative has the same form as the comparative. Unlike the comparative, however, which is nearly always used in the indefinite form, the superlative usually appears in the definite form, either with the use of ال or as the non-final term in a genitive construction, for example:

لي ستة أبناء، وماجد الأصغر
I have six children, and Majid is the youngest

لي ستة أبناء، وماجد أصغرهم
I have six children, and Majid is the youngest of them

لي ستة أبناء، وماجد أصغر ولد
I have six children, and Majid is the youngest child

لي ستة أبناء، وماجد أصغر الأولاد
I have six children, and Majid is the youngest of the children

Note that when used as comparatives and in genitive constructions, the same form is used with both masculine and feminine nouns, for example:

في رأيك ما هي أجمل مدينة في العالم العربي؟
in your opinion, what is the most beautiful city in the Arab world?

When used as an adjective after a feminine noun in conjunction with ال, however, the superlative takes a special form, فُعْلَى. This usage is particularly common in set phrases, for example:

الحرب الكبرى	القرون الوسطى
the Great War	the Middle Ages

6 CASE ENDINGS

Arabic has three cases, nominative (المرفوع), accusative (المنصوب) and genitive (المجرور). Cases are indicated by adding short vowels to nouns and adjectives:

	Definite	Indefinite
Nominative	الكتابُ **al-kitābu**	كتابٌ **kitābun**
Accusative	الكتابَ **al-kitāba**	كتاباً **kitāban**
Genitive	الكتابِ **al-kitābi**	كتابٍ **kitābin**

In singular and broken plural nouns and adjectives, cases are indicated by varying the *final* short vowels, as shown below:

	Definite singulars and broken plurals	Indefinite singulars and broken plurals
Nominative	الطالبُ	طالبٌ
	الأستاذةُ	أستاذةٌ
	الكتبُ	كتبٌ
Accusative	الطالبَ	طالباً
	الأستاذةَ	أستاذةً
	الكتبَ	كتباً
Genitive	الطالبِ	طالبٍ
	الأستاذةِ	أستاذةٍ
	الكتبِ	كتبٍ

In the dual and sound plural, cases are indicated by a change of the *penultimate* vowel. For example:

	Duals (definite and indefinite)	Sound plurals (definite and indefinite)
Nominative	مهندسان	مهندسون
	مصريتان	سودانيون
Accusative	مهندسَيْن	مهندسين
	مصريتَيْن	سودانيين
Genitive	مهندسَيْن	مهندسين
	سودانِيين	سودانِيين

In most variants of spoken Arabic case endings are not pronounced, and in most texts they are not written. The exception to this is the accusative ending on indefinite nouns known as **tanwīn al-fath** (ً) which changes the spelling of the word itself and can be seen in the example كتابًا **kitāban**. Case endings *are* written and pronounced in religious texts, classical literature and poetry, and play an important part in understanding Arabic grammar.

A. NOMINATIVE

The nominative case is used to indicate the subject of a sentence and is usually marked by the short vowel **damma** (with or without **tanwīn**) at the end of the word. Dual and sound plural human nouns take alternative endings, for example:

	Definite	Indefinite
Singular (m)	الولدُ	ولدٌ
	the boy	boy

Singular (f)	المدينة	مدينة
	the city	city
Dual	البيتان	بيتان
	the two houses	two houses
Human plural (m)	السودانيون	سودانيون
	the Sudanese	Sudanese
Human plural (f)	السوريات	سوريات
	the Syrians	Syrians

1 With possessive pronoun suffixes

When a possessive suffix is added to a nominative noun, the case ending appears between the noun and the suffix:

بيتُكَ	مدينتُها	صديقُهم
your house	her city	their friend

The one exception is when the first person singular possessive suffix ي is added, which causes the case ending to disappear:

بيتي	مدينتي
my house	my city

See also **Chapter 9, Section B.**

2 Use of the nominative case

In a sentence beginning with a noun, known as a nominal sentence, both the subject and the predicate (the word describing the subject) take nominative case endings:

البنتُ لبنانيةٌ	البيتُ كبيرٌ
the girl is Lebanese	the house is big
المهندسونَ جزائريونَ	الكتابان مملان
the engineers are Algerian	the two books are boring

In a sentence beginning with a verb, known as a verbal sentence, the subject of the sentence also takes a nominative case ending:

سافر الطالبُ إلى تركيا   الرجلُ يعمل في قطر

the student travelled to Turkey   **the man** works in Qatar

See also, **Chapter 17.**

B. ACCUSATIVE

The accusative case is used to indicate the object of the verb and is usually marked by the short vowel **fatha** (with or without **tanwīn**) at the end of the word. Dual and sound plural human nouns take alternative endings, as shown below:

	Definite	*Indefinite*
Singular (m)	الولدَ the boy	ولداً boy
Singular (f)	المدينةَ the city	مدينةً city
Dual	البيتَيْن the two houses	بيتَيْن two houses
Human plural (m)	السودانيِّين the Sudanese	سودانيِّين Sudanese
Human plural (f)	السوريات the Syrians	سوريات Syrians

1 With possessive pronoun suffixes

When a possessive suffix is added to an accusative noun, the case ending appears between the noun and the suffix:

بيتَكَ   مدينتَها   صديقَهم

your house   her city   their friend

The one exception is when the first person singular possessive suffix ي is added, which causes the case ending to disappear:

بيتي
my house

مدينتي
my city

See also **Chapter 9, Section B.**

2 Use of the accusative case
In a verbal sentence (*see* **Chapter 17, Section B**), the object of the verb takes an accusative case ending:

ضرب الرجلُ الولدَ
the man hit **the boy**

اشتريتُ كتاباً جديداً
I bought **a new book**

أكلت فاطمة تفاحاً
Fatima ate **an apple**

لم أقابل المدرسينَ المغربيِّينَ
I didn't meet **the Moroccan teachers**

Note that adverbs always take accusative endings (*see* **Chapter 7**):

جئتُ متأخراً
I came **late**

أحمد يحب السفرَ كثيراً
Ahmed likes travelling **a lot**

الولدُ يجري سريعاً
the boy runs **quickly**

نسكن قريباً من الجامعة
we live **close** to the university

3 With numbers
Nouns that occur after numbers between 11 and 99 are also accusative:

عمره ٢٨ سنةً
he is 28 **years** old

في هذا الصف ٦٣ طالباً
there are 36 **students** in this class

4 After إلا (except)
Nouns that occur after the word إلا (except) usually take the accusative ending:

لم أشترِ ألا كتاباً
I only bought one **book**

جاء كل الطلاب إلا طالباً
all the students came except **one**

5 'Absolute accusative'

Note the use of the accusative in the following sentences to emphasize or qualify a verb:

كرهت دراستها كرهاً شديداً
she really hated her studies

أدرس العربية حباً بها
I study Arabic because I like it

C. GENITIVE

The genitive case is used to indicate possession and is usually marked by the short vowel **kasra** at the end of the word. Dual and sound human plural nouns take alternative endings, as shown below:

	Definite	Indefinite
Singular (m)	الولد the boy	ولد boy
Singular (f)	المدينة the city	مدينة city
Dual	البيتَيْن the two houses	بيتَيْن two houses
Human plural (m)	السودانيِّين the Sudanese	سودانيِّين Sudanese
Human plural (f)	السوريات the Syrians	سوريات Syrians

1 With possessive pronoun suffixes

When a possessive suffix is added to a genitive noun, the case ending appears between the noun and the suffix:

بيتك
your house

مدينتها
her city

صديقنا
their friend

The genitive ending also affects the pronunciation of the
following possessive suffixes:

كتابه **kitābihi** سيارتهما **sayyāratihimā** أقاربهم **aqāribihim**
his book their car *(dual)* their relatives

When the first person singular possessive suffix ي is added, it
causes the case ending to disappear:

بيتي مدينتي
my house my city

2 Use of the genitive case

a) After a preposition (*see also* Chapter 12):

أذهب إلى السوق تسكن في بيت صغير
I'm going to **the market** she lives in **a small house**

وضع الفنجانَ على الطاولة
he put the coffee cup on **the table**

تعرفت على طلاب سودانيّينَ
I got to know **some Sudanese students**

سافرنا إلى اليمن لإجازة هذا الكتابُ يتكلم عن التاريخ
we travelled to Yemen for **a holiday** this book talks about **history**

b) In an **idāfa** construction (*see also* Chapter 4, Section E):
The first noun in an **idāfa** construction takes a case ending
appropriate to its function in the sentence, but the subsequent
nouns are always genitive:

وزارةُ التربية محطةُ القطار
the Ministry of **Education** the **train** station

رأيتُ صاحبَ البيت
(*lit.* I saw the owner of the **house**) I saw the landlord

يدرس في كلية الحقوق
he studies in the Faculty of **Law**

D. DIPTOTES

There are several groups of nouns and adjectives, known as diptotes, which do not follow the rules given above in their indefinite forms. Diptotes do not take **tanwīn** and are marked by a **ḍamma** in the nominative and by a **fatḥa** in both the accusative and genitive. When made definite by ال or an **iḍāfa** construction, the **kasra** reappears in the genitive. The main groups are as follows:

1 Some patterns of broken plurals

أساليب	كنائس	مساجد
styles	churches	mosques

2 Adjectives which follow the pattern أفعل, including comparatives and superlatives, and some colours

أجمل	أحسن	أكثر
prettier	better	more
أزرق	أحمر	أبيض
red	blue	white

3 Adjectives with the pattern فعلان

عطشان	جوعان	غضبان
thirsty	hungry	angry

4 Female names

فاطمة	زينب
Fatima	Zaynab

5 Many place names

حلب	بيروت	دمشقَ
Aleppo	Beirut	Damascus

6 Place names formed by joining two nouns

بيت لحم	حضرموت
Bethlehem	Hadramawt

7 Nouns ending with ء

أصدقاء	صحراء
friends	desert

8 Nouns ending with ى

مقهى	مرضى
café	sick people

The following table shows the case endings for these groups of nouns and adjectives when they are indefinite:

	Nominative	*Accusative*	*Genitive*
Group 1	مساجدُ	مساجدَ	مساجدَ
Group 2	أحمرُ	أحمرَ	أحمرَ
Group 3	غضبانُ	غضبانَ	غضبانَ
Group 4	زينبُ	زينبَ	زينبَ
Group 5	دمشقُ	دمشقَ	دمشقَ
Group 6	حضرموتُ	حضرموتَ	حضرموتَ
Group 7	صحراءُ	صحراءَ	صحراءَ
Group 8	مقهىً	مقهىً	مقهىً

 E. THE FIVE NOUNS

There is a group of five nouns, known as الأسماء الخمسة, which behave
differently when case endings are added. These five nouns are:

أب	أخ	حَم
father	brother	father-in-law

فو	ذو
mouth	possessor of

When used in an **idāfa** construction or with a possessive suffix, the
spelling of these five nouns changes according to the case:

	Nominative	Accusative	Genitive
'father'	أبو	أبا	أبي
'brother'	أخو	أخا	أخي
'father-in-law'	حمو	حما	حمي
'mouth'	فو	فا	في
'possessor of'	ذو	ذا	ذي

أخوها يدرس الطب
her brother studies medicine

ضربت زينب أخاها
Zeinab hit her brother

ذهبت إلى بيت أخيها
I went to her brother's house

7 ADVERBS

Arabic has relatively few adverbs in comparison with most European languages. Adverbial expressions can, however, be formed in a number of different ways.

1 Adjectives or nouns with accusative endings

The most common way of expressing an adverb is by adding the accusative ending to an adjective. As in English, the position of an adverb in Arabic is flexible, although it usually comes after the verb it modifies rather than before it:

| حمزة يعزف الكمان جيداً | تزور سوسن عائلتها كثيراً |
| Hamza plays the violin well | Sawsan visits her family a lot |

جرت العداءة البحرينية رقية الغسرة سريعاً في أولمبياد بكين
the Bahraini sprinter Ruqaya al-Ghasra ran quickly in the Beijing Olympics

Many common adverbs, particularly of time, also have an indefinite accusative form:

أنا دائماً مشغولٍ	عدنان أستاذ أيضاً
أنا مشغول دائماً	عدنان أيضاً أستاذ
I am always busy	Adnan is also a teacher

2 ب + noun

Another common way of expressing an adverb is to combine a noun with the preposition ب (with):

جرى العداء بسرعة	نجح في الامتحان بسهولة
(*lit.* the sprinter ran with speed)	(*lit.* he passed the exam with ease)
the sprinter ran quickly	he passed the exam easily

3 بشكل + adjective

This construction translates as 'in a ... way' and can be used instead of an adverb:

مات فهد لأنه ساق السيارة بشكل خطير

(*lit.* Fahd died because he drove the car in a dangerous way)

Fahd died because he drove the car dangerously

لا يريد علي أن يحل المشكلة بشكل عنيف

(*lit.* Ali doesn't want to solve the problem in a violent way)

Ali doesn't want to solve the problem violently

4 Object phrases

See also **Chapter 17, Section B.**

Object phrases are formed with a verb + its verbal noun + an adjective. Both the verbal noun and the adjective must be in the accusative case:

نام نوماً ثقيلاً

(*lit.* he slept a deep sleep)

he slept heavily

ضرب الملاكم خصمه ضرباً شديداً

(*lit.* the boxer hit his opponent a hard hit)

the boxer hit his opponent hard

8 PERSONAL PRONOUNS

Personal pronouns refer to people or things (I, you, he, she, it *etc*).

Person	Singular		Dual		Plural	
1st	أَنا	I	نَحْنُ	we**	نَحْنُ	we
2nd	أَنْتَ	you *(m)*	أَنْتُما	you *(m/f)*	أَنْتُم	you *(m)*
	أَنْتِ	you *(f)*			أَنْتُنَّ	you *(f)*
3rd	هُوَ	he, it	هُما	they *(m/f)*	هُم	they *(m)*
	هِيَ	she, it, they*			هُنَّ	they *(f)*

* For non-human plurals.

** There is no separate dual form for the first person.

1   With non-human nouns

The 3rd person singular personal pronouns هو (he, it) and
هي (she, it) can also be used to refer to non-human nouns,
depending on their gender:

عندي بيت. هو كبير
I have a house. It's big

أين مدينة دمشق؟ هي في سورية
where is Damascus? It's in Syria

The 3rd person dual pronoun هما (they) can also be used to refer
to groups of two non-human nouns:

اشتريتُ كتابين. هما كتابان ممتازان
I bought two books. They are excellent books

Non-human plurals are treated as singular and feminine, so are
referred to using هي (they):

هم أساتذة مصريون

they are Egyptian teachers

هل الطالبات لبنانيات؟ لا، هنَّ أردنيات

are the students *(f)* Lebanese? No, they're Jordanian

في بيتي ثلاث غرف. هي غرف صغيرة

there are three rooms in my house. They are small rooms

> Note
>
> The 3rd person plural pronouns هم and هنَّ (they) can only be
> used for plural human nouns. هنَّ refers to female-only groups
> and هم refers to both male-only and mixed groups. Non-human
> plurals must be referred to using the 3rd person feminine
> singular personal pronoun هي.

2 Before a verb

When a personal pronoun appears before a verb in English,
it can be omitted in Arabic. The subject of the verb should be
obvious from the form of the verb or the context:

هو أستاذ في جامعة القاهرة. يدرِّس الهندسة

he is a teacher at Cairo University. (He) teaches engineering

السودانيون يحبون الفول كثيراً. يأكلونه يومياً

the Sudanese like beans a lot. (They) eat them every day

In texts where the short vowels are not written, omitting a
personal pronoun can cause confusion. The example below could
refer to the 1st, 2nd or 3rd person feminine singular and the
subject can only be identified from the wider context:

خرجت من البيت وذهبت إلى السوق

I/you *(m)*/you *(f)*/she left the house and went to the market

9 OBJECT AND POSSESSIVE PRONOUNS

A. OBJECT PRONOUNS

Object pronouns are used when the pronoun is the object of the verb. In Arabic object pronouns appear in the form of suffixes added to the verb.

Person	Singular		Dual		Plural	
1st	ـني	me	ـنا	us two*	ـنا	us
2nd	ـكَ	you (m)	ـكُما	you (m/f)	ـكُم	you (m)
	ـكِ	you (f)			ـكُنّ	you (f)
3rd	ـهُ	him, it	ـهُما	them (m/f)	ـهُم	them (m)
	ـها	her, it, them			ـهُنّ	them (f)

* There is no separate dual form for the first person.

عفواً هل يمكنك أن تساعدني؟
excuse me, can you help me?

رأيتها وهي جالسة في الحديقة
I saw her sitting in the garden

طلبت قهوة ولكن لم أشربها
I ordered a coffee but didn't drink it

كان الولد يبكي لأن أخته ضربته
the boy was crying because his sister hit him

OBJECT AND POSSESSIVE PRONOUNS

1 With the plural ending وا
When object pronouns are added to the plural ending وا the final
ا is removed from the verb:

أصدقائي لا يستطيعون أن يساعدوني مع هذه المشاكل
my friends can't help me with these problems

حاولت نانسي أن تتكلم بالعربية مع التونسيين ولكن ما فهموها جيداً
Nancy tried to speak Arabic with the Tunisians, but they didn't
understand her

2 With non-human nouns
The object pronouns هـ (him, it) and ها (her, it) can be used to
refer to non-human singular objects:

بحثت عن المتحف ولكن لم أجده
I searched for the museum but didn't find it

هذه سيارتنا. اشتريناها أمس
this is our car. We bought it yesterday

3 With human nouns
Human plural objects take the plural suffixes هُم and هُنَّ (them).
Non-human plural objects are treated as singular and feminine,
and take the singular ها suffix:

قابلناهم في المطار
we met them *(m)* at the airport

عندي كتب كثيرة ولكن لم أقرأها كلها بعد
I have many books, but I haven't read them all yet

4 Vowels
The vowel of the third person suffixes changes from a **damma** to
a **kasra** if the suffix is preceded by another **kasra** or a ي.

سَيَبْنِيه
he will build it

B. POSSESSIVE PRONOUNS

Possessive pronouns are used to show ownership or similar relationships. They appear as suffixes added to the relevant noun. Except in the 1st person singular, they are identical to the object pronouns:

Person	Singular		Dual		Plural	
1st	ـي	my	ـنا	our*	ـنا	our
2nd	ـكَ	your (m)	ـكُما	your (m/f)	ـكُم	your (m)
	ـكِ	your (f)			ـكُنَّ	your (f)
3rd	ـهُ	his, its	ـهُما	their (m/f)	ـهُم	their (m)
	ـها	her, its			ـهُنَّ	their (f)

* Arabic does not have a separate dual form for the first person.

أختي تسكن مع زوجها في بيتنا
my sister lives with her husband in our house

أحمد وفاطمة يسكنان معاً وبيتهما صغير
Ahmed and Fatima live together. Their house is small

1 With nouns ending in ة

If a noun ends in ة, this becomes (and is pronounced as) ت when a possessive pronoun is attached:

أظنّ أنّ مدينتهم أحسن من مدينتنا
I think that their city is better than our city

هل هذه سيارتك؟ لا، تلك سيارتي
is this your car? No, that is my car

2 With prepositions

Possessive pronoun suffixes can be also be used with
prepositions, for example معي (with me), فوقه (above it), دونها
(without her). *See also* **Chapter 12**.

The combination of certain prepositions with the appropriate
possessive suffix also provides the most common way of
expressing possession in Arabic. This construction can be
translated using the English verb 'to have'.

a) عِنْد

This preposition is used with the possessive pronoun suffixes to
refer to items which can be physically possessed:

عندي سيارة	عندها كتاب جديد
I have a car	she has a new book

والدي ووالدتي عندهما بيت كبير
my father and mother have a large house

It can also be used to refer to certain abstract concepts:

عندي سؤال	هل عندكم وقت؟
I have a question	do you have time?

This type of construction is negated using ليس, or less formally
with ما:

ما عندنا وقت اليوم	ليس عنده كمبيوتر
We don't have time today	he doesn't have a computer

See also **Chapter 15, Section A.**

b) لِ

Possessive pronoun suffixes can be added to the preposition لِ to
refer to human relationships:

لي أخت تسكن في اليمن
I have a sister who lives in Yemen

نادية لها ابن وبنتان
Nadia has a son and two daughters

محمود له أصدقاء كثيرون من أصل إنجليزي
Mahmoud has a lot of English friends

ل can also be used to refer to the possession of abstract concepts:

هذه المدينة لها تاريخ مثير
this city has an exciting history

This type of construction is also negated using ما or ليس:

عمار ليس له أخت
Ammar doesn't have a sister

ندى ما لها أطفال
Nada doesn't have any children

c) مَع

Possessive pronoun suffixes can be added to the preposition مع
(with) to refer to possessions physically with the person at the
time of speech:

عفواً، هل معك قلم؟
excuse me, do you have a pen?

ما معي ريال ولكن معي دينار
I don't have riyals but I have dinars

d) في

When referring to non-human subjects possessing things, the
preposition في is used with a possessive pronoun:

فندق أكروبول في الخرطوم فيه خمسون غرفةً ومسبح وثلاثة مطاعم
the Hotel Acropole in Khartoum has fifty rooms, a swimming pool and
three restaurants

مدينة كسلا فيها مقاه عديدة ولكن ليس فيها مقهى إنترنت
the city of Kassala has many cafés but no internet cafés

See also **Chapter 12.**

3 **With the 'sisters of إِنَّ'**

Pronoun suffixes can also be added to the particles known as the 'sisters of إِنَّ' (*see* **Chapter 17, Section A**).

هي غائبة اليوم لأنها مريضة

she's absent today because she's ill

مدينة الخرطوم جميلة لكنّها مزدحمة

Khartoum is beautiful, but it's crowded

قالت إنها ستأتي متأخراً   علي يعتقد أنّني مجنون

she said she'll arrive late   Ali thinks that I am mad

كان محمود يتمشى كأنه سكران

Mahmoud was walking as if he was drunk

10 RELATIVE PRONOUNS

Relative pronouns introduce a relative clause, a phrase which is generally, though not always, used to provide further information about a noun. In English, words such as 'which', 'that', 'who' and 'what' are all relative pronouns.

The use of relative pronouns in Arabic is somewhat different from in English, and varies according to whether the noun referred to is definite or indefinite (*see* **Chapter 4**).

A. INDEFINITE NOUNS

If the noun being described is indefinite, no relative pronoun is needed to introduce the relative clause. For example:

هي طالبة تدرس اللغة الروسية
(*lit.* she is a student studies Russian)
she is a student who studies Russian

أعرف رجلاً يسكن في الجزائر
(*lit.* I know a man lives in Algiers)
I know a man who lives in Algiers

The relative clause ('who studies Russian', 'who lives in Algiers' *etc*) should make sense in Arabic as if it were a separate sentence. If the noun referred to is not the subject of the verb in the relative clause, an object pronoun referring back to the noun must be added to the sentence. For example:

أمس شاهدت فيلماً استمتعت به
(*lit.* yesterday I watched a film I enjoyed it)
yesterday I watched a film that I enjoyed

هذه مقالة أريد أن أقرأها
(*lit.* this is an article I want to read it)
this is an article that I want to read

B. DEFINITE NOUNS

If the noun being described is definite, the appropriate relative pronoun must be used.

	Singular	*Dual*		*Plural*
		nom	acc/gen	
Masculine	الَّذي	اللذانِ	اللذَيْنِ	الَّذينَ
Feminine	الَّتي	اللتانِ	اللتَيْنِ	اللاتي / اللواتي / اللائي*

* All three forms are used, although in modern Arabic اللواتي is probably the most common.

The relative pronoun must agree with the noun it is referring to in gender and number (as well as, in the dual, in case):

تعرفت على المرأة التي تسكن في ذلك البيت
I got to know the woman who lives in that house

هذا هو الأستاذ الذي يدرّس اللغة العربية
this is the professor who teaches Arabic

هما الطالبتان اللتان تدرسان في جامعة أم درمان الإسلامية
these are the two students *(f)* who study at Umdurman Islamic University

الشرطة لم تجد المجرمين الذين سرقوا سيارتي
the police haven't found the criminals who stole my car

رأيت البنتين اللتين تعرفت عليهما في القاهرة
I saw the two girls whom I got to know in Cairo

Note that non-human plurals, as usual, are treated as feminine singular:

أريد أن أذبح الكلاب التي تنبح طوال الليل
I want to kill the dogs that bark all night

قرأ أكرم كل الكتب التي اشتراها في المكتبة
Akram read all the books that he bought in the bookshop

As with indefinite nouns, the relative clause should make sense in Arabic as if it were a separate sentence. Sometimes, an object pronoun referring back to the noun needs to be added to the sentence:

أين الكتاب الذي اشتريته أمس؟
(*lit.* where is the book that I bought it yesterday?)
where is the book that I bought yesterday?

البنت التي تعرفت عليها في السوق من أصل سوداني
(*lit.* the girl who I met her in the market is of Sudanese origin)
the girl who I met in the market is of Sudanese origin

C. GENERAL RELATIVE PRONOUNS

1 ما **(what, whatever, the thing that)**

If the noun referred to in the relative clause is not stated, ما can be used as the relative pronoun:

لا يعرف ما يريد
he doesn't know what he wants

If ما is followed by a verb which requires a preposition, an object pronoun is needed:

والدها يعطيها كل ما تحتاج إليه
(*lit.* her father gives her all that she needs it)
her father gives her whatever she needs

2 مَن (who, whoever, the person who)

If the person referred to in the relative clause is not stated, مَن can be used as the relative pronoun:

عمر يتكلم مع من يريد

Amr talks to whoever he likes

If مَن is followed by a verb which requires a preposition, an object pronoun is needed:

فريدة تتكلم مع مَن يستمع إليها

(*lit.* Farida talks to whoever will listen to her)

Farida talks to whoever will listen

11 DEMONSTRATIVES

Demonstratives are words such as 'this', 'these', 'that' and 'those' in English. They can be used as both pronouns and adjectives.

A. 'THIS' AND 'THESE'

	Singular	Dual		Plural
		nom	acc/gen	
Masculine	هذا	هذانِ	هذَينِ	هؤُلاء (m/f)
Feminine	هذِهِ	هاتانِ	هاتَينِ	

1 As an adjective

Each form given in the table above can be used as a demonstrative adjective to point out a particular person or thing. The form used must agree with the noun to which it refers in gender, number and (when dual) in case. Non-human plurals are treated as feminine singular.

When the demonstrative is used in this way, the noun must be made definite by using the definite article الـ:

هذا الولد
this boy

هؤُلاء الطلاب
these students

هذه الأشجار
these trees

هذه السيارات
these cars

هذان البيتان
these two houses

هاتان البنتان
these two girls

أحمد اشترى هذين البيتين
Ahmed bought these two houses

When a demonstrative is used as an adjective to describe the non-final term in an **idāfa** construction or a proper noun, the demonstrative comes last:

باب البيت هذا

this door of the house

2 As a pronoun

The demonstratives given above can also be used as pronouns in nominal sentences (*see* **Chapter 17, Section A**):

هذه جامعةٌ	هذا كتابٌ
this is a university	this is a book
هؤْلاء أساتذة	هذا باب البيت
these (people) are teachers	this is a door of the house

When a demonstrative pronoun is used in this way with a definite noun, it is usually followed by the relevant 3rd person personal pronoun, which acts as a link:

هؤْلاء هم الأساتذة	هذه هي الجامعة	هذا هو الكتاب
these are the teachers	this is the university	this is the book
هذا هو أحمد		هذا هو باب البيت
this is Ahmed		this is the door of the house

B. 'THAT' AND 'THOSE'

ذَلك is used with masculine singular nouns.

تِلك is used with feminine singular nouns and non-human plurals.

أُوْلَئِك is used with human plurals, both masculine and feminine.

1 As an adjective

Each different form of ذَلك (that, those) can be used as an adjective to point out a particular person or thing, further away than something pointed out using one of the variants of هذا (*see*

Section A). The form used must agree with the noun to which it refers in both gender and number. The noun must also be definite:

أولئك الطلاب	تلك المدينة	ذلك الكتاب
those students	that city	that book

Non-human plurals are treated as feminine singular:

تلك الكلاب	تلك السنوات
those dogs	those years

When a demonstrative is used as an adjective in an **idāfa** construction or to describe a proper noun, the demonstrative comes last:

باب البيت ذلك
that door of the house

2 As a pronoun

The same forms of ذلك can be used as a pronoun with an indefinite noun:

أولئك مهندسون	ذلك فيلٌ
those are engineers	that is an elephant

تلك كنيسةٌ	ذلك باب البيت
that is a church	that is a door of the house

When ذلك is used as a pronoun with a definite noun, it is usually followed by the relevant 3rd person personal pronoun:

أولئك هم المهندسون	ذلك هو الفيل
those are the engineers	that is the elephant

تلك هي الكنيسة	ذلك هو باب البيت
that is the church	that is the door of the house

12 PREPOSITIONS

Like English, Arabic has many prepositions, known as حروف الجر.
Most are individual words, although some prepositions consist of a
single letter joined onto a following noun.

Most Arabic prepositions have loose English equivalents, although
there are several cases where the usage is different. Certain verbs
are only found in combination with certain prepositions, and in
some cases, changing the preposition can give the verb a different
meaning. There are too many of these verbs to list here, although
some of the most common are shown in the examples. A good
Arabic dictionary should list which specific prepositions, if any,
follow the verb.

Note that nouns that follow prepositions *always* take the genitive
case.

A. COMMON PREPOSITIONS

1 في

a) في (in)

يسكن علي في بيت كبير
Ali lives in a big house

القاهرة أكبر مدينة في الشرق الأوسط
Cairo is the biggest city in the Middle East

b) في (at)

هند تدرس في جامعة بيرزيت
Hind studies at Birzeit University

عادةً آكل الفطور في الساعة الثامنة
I usually eat breakfast at 8 o'clock

c) في with pronoun suffixes

The preposition في can also be used to indicate possession when referring to non-human nouns. *See also* **Chapter 9, Section B.**

فندق هيلتون فيه ثلاثة مطاعم

(*lit.* the Hilton Hotel has in it three restaurants)
the Hilton Hotel has three restaurants

المدينة التي أسكن فيها صغيرة جداً

(*lit.* the city that I live in it is very small)
the city that I live in is very small

d) في with certain verbs

نجح سمير في الامتحان   نوال ترغب في الدراسة في عمان

Samir passed the exam   Nawal wants to study in Amman

بسبب البطالة، أحمد يفكّر في الهجرة إلى أمريكا

because of unemployment, Ahmed is thinking of emigrating to America

2 مِن

a) مِن (from)

يوسف طالب من السودان   عزيزة من أصل مصري

Yusuf is a student from Sudan   Aziza is of Egyptian origin

مكتب تسجيل الأجانب مفتوح من الساعة العاشرة صباحاً

the Aliens' Registration Office is open from 10 o'clock in the morning

Note the following use of مِن to indicate location:

تقع مدينة درم قريباً من البحر

the city of Durham is located close to the sea

b) مِن (than)

مِن can be used to make comparisons:

أحب القهوة أكثر من الشاي

I like coffee more than tea

في رأي دِمَشق أجمل من حَلَب

in my opinion, Damascus is more beautiful than Aleppo

c) من (among, including)

ابن بطوطة سافر إلى بلدان عديدة، منها اليمن ومصر وتونس

Ibn Battuta travelled to many countries, among them Yemen, Egypt and Tunisia

d) من with certain verbs

أخيراً انتهى من كتابة الرواية

he finally finished writing the novel

بنت الصحن طبق يمني يتكون من الخبز والعسل والزبدة

Bint as-Sahn is a Yemeni dish consisting of bread, honey and butter

3 إلى

a) إلى (to)

جاء خالد إلى الصف متأخراً

Khalid came late to class

في العطلة سافرت مريم إلى الصين

in the holidays, Maryam travelled to China

b) When object pronouns are added to إلى, the ى becomes a ي:

هل تستمع إلى الراديو؟ نعم، أستمع إليه كثيراً

do you listen to the radio? Yes, I listen to it a lot

قال «هذا هو السارق» وكان يشير إليَّ!

he said, 'this is the thief', and pointed to me!

c) إلى with certain verbs

أنا تعبان وأحتاج إلى شرب القهوة

I'm tired and need to drink coffee

4 لِ

This preposition is a single letter, and joins onto the following noun.

a) لِ (for)

اشتريت هدية لوالدتي
I bought a present for my mother

b) لِ (in order to)

لِ can also be used with a present tense subjunctive verb or a verbal noun to indicate purpose. *See also* **Chapter 13, Sections C** *and* **F.**

يذهب عمار إلى المكتبة للدراسة
Ammar is going to the library (in order) to study

جاءت فوز إلى لندن لتتعلم اللغة الإنجليزية
Fawz came to London (in order) to learn English

c) لِ with certain verbs

لم يسمح الأستاذ للطلاب بالخروج مبكراً
the teacher did not allow the students to leave early

5 عَلى

a) عَلى (on)

وضعتُ المجلةَ على الطاولة
I put the magazine on the table

تقع أم درمان على الضفة الغربية لنهر النيل
Omdurman is located on the west bank of the Nile

b) When object pronouns are added to على، the ى becomes a ي:

الكرسي مكسور فلا تجلس عليه
the chair's broken so don't sit on it

في الزلزال انهار البيت علينا
in the earthquake, the house collapsed on us

c) على used with certain verbs

حصلت سعاد على الدكتوراه في السنة الماضية
Souad obtained her doctorate last year

شجعت صديقتي على السفر إلى الخارج
I encouraged my friend to travel abroad

6 عَن

a) عَن (about)

قرأتُ كتاباً ممتازاً عَن تاريخ العراق
I read an excellent book about the history of Iraq

يحب صديقي الإنجليزي أن يتكلم عن الجو
my English friend likes to talk about the weather

b) عَن (from)

تختلف اللهجة الشامية عن اللهجة المغربية كثيراً
the Syrian dialect differs from the Moroccan dialect a lot

غابت فريدة عن كل محاضراتها هذا الأسبوع
Farida was absent from all her lectures this week

محمود هو شخصٌ مزعجٌ وأحاول أن أبتعد عنه
Mahmoud is an annoying person, and I try to stay away from him

c) عَن with certain verbs

ما استطاع أحد أن يجيب عَن السؤال الصعب
nobody could answer the difficult question

قرر خالد أن يتوقّف عن التدخين
Khalid decided to quit smoking

d) When عَن is used with the question words ما (what) and مَن (who), the two words combine in the following ways:

عَمَّ؟ = ما + عن
about what?

عَمَّن؟ = مَن + عَن
about whom?

عَمَّ يتكلم ذلك الفيلم؟
what's that film about?

عَمَّن يتكلم الأستاذ؟
who's the teacher talking about?

7 مَع

a) مَع (with)

مَع is used to mean 'with' when referring to people:

ذهب يحيى إلى النادي مع صديقه
Yahya went to the club with his friend

خواطر تحب لعب الشطرنج مع أخيها
Khawatir likes playing chess with her brother

b) مَع with pronoun suffixes

Object pronoun suffixes can be added to مَع to refer to objects that are physically with the possessor:

هل مَعكَ قلم؟
(*lit.* is a pen with you?)
do you have a pen?

اليوم ليس مَعي فلوس
(*lit.* there is no money with me)
today I have no money

See also **Chapter 9, Section B.**

8 بِ

This preposition is a single letter, and joins onto the following noun.

a) بِ (with)

بِ is used to mean 'with' when referring to non-human nouns:

السودانيون يشربون القهوة بالزنجبيل
the Sudanese drink coffee with ginger

تماضر مشغولة بكتابة بحثها

Tamadur is busy with writing her thesis

b) بـ (by)

سافرتُ إلى وادي حلفا بالقطار

I travelled to Wadi Halfa by train

كتبَت الرواية بقلم نجيب محفوظ

the novel was written by (the pen of) Naguib Mahfouz

عادةَ عبد الملك يذهب إلى المكتبة بالسيارة

'Abdul-Malik usually goes to the library by car

c) بـ (in)

كتب العنوان بالحروف العربيَة

he wrote the address in Arabic letters

كانوا يتكلمون باللغة الكردية

they were speaking in Kurdish

d) بـ with certain verbs

شعرت لواحظ بالخجل عندما التقت بماجد

Lawahiz felt shy when she met Majed

هل تستمتعين بالرقص الشرقي، يا ريم؟

do you enjoy belly dancing, Reem?

بعد التخرج، يريد سامي أن يلتحق بالجيش

after graduating, Sami wants to join the army

اتصل ياسر بوالده ولكنه لم يرد

Yasser called his father but he didn't answer

كيف علمتَ بموت الرئيس السوري؟

how did you learn of the death of the Syrian president?

لا تسمح الحكومة للسائحين بدخول السودان بدون تأشيرة

the government doesn't allow tourists to enter Sudan without a visa

9 حَتَّى (until, till)

في شهر رمضان، يصوم المسلمون من الفجر حَتَّى الغسق

in the month of Ramadan, Muslims fast from dawn until dusk

ركبنا القطار حَتَّى مدينة عطبرة

we took the train as far as the town of Atbara

10 ك (as, like)

This preposition is a single letter, and joins onto the noun that follows it:

كان الجندي شجاعاً كالأسد

the soldier was brave like a lion/the soldier was as brave as a lion

انطلق كالسهم

(*lit.* he ran like an arrow)

he ran like the wind

11 مُنْذُ (since, ago, for)

أنا أكره شرب الشاي بالحليب منذ طفولتي

I have hated drinking tea with milk since my childhood

يدرس عثمان اللغة الألمانية منذ خمس سنوات

Uthman has studied German for five years

B. ADVERBIAL EXPRESSIONS OF TIME AND PLACE

As we saw in **Chapter 7**, Arabic does not have many adverbs. Instead, many adverbial expressions used to describe time and place are formed with prepositions followed by a noun in the genitive (*see* **Chapter 6, Section C**). Those relating to time are known as ظروف الزمان, while those relating to place are known as ظروف المكان.

1 Prepositions relating to time

Among the most common prepositions relating to time are:

before	قبل	after	بعد
during	خلال	throughout	طوال

بعد المحاضرة شربنا القهوة في المقهى
after the lecture, we drank coffee in the café

كانت الحياة في بغداد صعبة خلال التسعينات
life was difficult in Baghdad during the 90s

قبل الوصول إلى كسلا، مات حسام في حادث سيارة
before he got to Kassala, Hussam died in a car accident

الجو في بورسودان حار جداً طوال السنة
the weather in Port Sudan is very hot throughout the year

2 Prepositions relating to place

Among the most common prepositions relating to place are:

above	فوق	between	بين
below	تحت	outside	خارج
next to	جنب	inside	داخل
behind	وراء	across	عبر
in front of	أمام	opposite	مقابل

There are also some compound adverbs of place, formed by combining two prepositions:

من بين	بجانب
among	next to

تقع مدينة أم درمان مقابل الخرطوم عبر نهر النيل
Umdurman is situated accross the Nile from Khartoum

يقع البنك بين المكتبة والمسرح بجانب البلدية
the bank is located between the library and the theatre, next to the town hall

وُضعَت قنبلة تحت سيارة الرئيس
a bomb was placed under the president's car

المسجد الأموي أمام سوق الحامدية في دمشق
the Umayyad Mosque is in front of Souq al-Hamidiyyeh in Damascus

13 THE VERB

A. BASIC PRINCIPLES

Arabic verbs are based on different patterns of vowels used in conjunction with three (occasionally four) root letters, (see **Chapter 2**). They are conjugated for person and number through the use of prefixes and suffixes.

Although the system may appear complex at first, it is in fact surprisingly regular. For example, the suffix used in the 1st person singular past tense is used throughout the verbal system.

There are two main tenses in Arabic, the perfect (or past) tense and the imperfect (or present) tense. The perfect tense is used to describe completed actions and the imperfect tense is used to describe ongoing actions. Note that there is no infinitive form of the verb in Arabic.

Arabic verbs can be divided into two groups: 'simple verbs' (also known as Form I verbs) and 'derived form verbs'.

B. SIMPLE VERBS – PERFECT TENSE

Simple verbs are based on a pattern in the 3rd person masculine singular of the perfect tense as follows:

Consonant + **fatha** + consonant + vowel + consonant + **fatha**

Note that the middle vowel can be a **fatha**, **kasra** or **damma**, as in:

كَتَبَ	شَرِبَ	سَهُلَ
write	drink	be easy

The 3rd person singular form of the perfect tense (eg كَتَبَ 'he wrote', بنى 'he built' *etc*) is regarded as the basic form of the verb and verbs are listed in this form in almost all dictionaries. The different forms of the verb in the perfect tense are as follows:

1st singular	كَتَبْتُ	I wrote, I have written
2nd singular *(m)*	كَتَبْتَ	you wrote, you have written
2nd singular *(f)*	كَتَبْتِ	you wrote, you have written
3rd singular *(m)*	كَتَبَ	he wrote, he has written
3rd singular *(f)*	كَتَبَتْ	she wrote, she has written
2nd dual	كَتَبْتُمَا	you wrote, you have written
3rd dual *(m)*	كَتَبَا	they wrote, they have written
3rd dual *(f)*	كَتَبَتَا	they wrote, they have written
1st plural	كَتَبْنَا	we wrote, we have written
2nd plural *(m)*	كَتَبْتُم	you wrote, you have written
2nd plural *(f)*	كَتَبْتُنَّ	you wrote, you have written
3rd plural *(m)*	كَتَبوا	they wrote, they have written
3rd plural *(f)*	كَتَبْنَ	they wrote, they have written

The perfect tense is most commonly used for actions or states in the past, with a range of meanings covering both the English simple past ('he wrote' *etc*) and past perfect ('he has written' *etc*). It is also used in conditional sentences (*see* **Chapter 17, Section F**). It may be negated using ما, though in modern formal Arabic this usage has been largely replaced by the jussive (*see* **Section C**).

ما شربوا الخمر
they did not drink wine

ما كتب الرسالة
he did not write the letter

To emphasize the completed nature of the action or state indicated by the verb, the particle قَدْ (sometimes translated as 'already') may be used, as in:

قد ذهب الى المحطَة
he's gone to the station

C. IMPERFECT TENSE

The imperfect tense is mainly used to describe the present. It has three forms: indicative, subjunctive, and jussive.

1 Imperfect indicative

The imperfect indicative is the most basic of the imperfect tenses, at least in terms of meaning. Its forms are as follows:

1st singular	أَكْتُبُ	I write, I am writing, I will write
2nd singular (m)	تَكْتُبُ	you write, you are writing, you will write
2nd singular (f)	تَكْتُبِينَ	you write, you are writing, you will write
3rd singular (m)	يَكْتُبُ	he writes, he is writing, he will write
3rd singular (f)	تَكْتُبُ	she writes, she is writing, she will write
2nd dual	تَكْتُبانِ	you write, you are writing, you will write
3rd dual (m)	يَكْتُبانِ	they write, they are writing, they will write
3rd dual (f)	تَكْتُبانِ	they write, they are writing, they will write
1st plural	نَكْتُبُ	we write, we are writing, we will write
2nd plural (m)	تَكْتُبونَ	you write, you are writing, you will write
2nd plural (f)	تَكْتُبْنَ	you write, you are writing, you will write
3rd plural (m)	يَكْتُبونَ	they write, they are writing, they will write

| 3rd plural (f) | يَكْتُبْنَ | they write, they are writing, they will write |

Note that, as in the past tense, the middle vowel may be either a
fatha, **kasra** or **damma**:

| يَكْتُبُ | يَشْرَبُ | يَسْهُلُ |
| write | drink | be easy |

As the relationship between the middle vowels of the past and
present tenses is unpredictable, each one should be learnt separately
until patterns become apparent.

Like the past tense, the imperfect indicative covers a range of English
meanings including, for example, 'I write', 'I am writing', 'I do write',
'I shall write' *etc.* Where it is necessary explicitly to indicate the
future, the verb is preceded by سَ (joined to the verb) or, for greater
emphasis سَوْفَ. The present negative is expressed with لا.

سيأكل السمك
he will eat the fish

سوف أقتلك!
I will kill you! *(emphatic)*

لا تفهم العربية
she doesn't understand Arabic

2 Imperfect subjunctive and jussive

The subjunctive and jussive forms of the imperfect tense are as
follows:

a) Subjunctive

1st singular	أَكْتُبَ	I may write
2nd singular (m)	تَكْتُبَ	you may write
2nd singular (f)	تَكْتُبِي	you may write
3rd singular (m)	يَكْتُبَ	he may write

3rd singular (f)	تَكْتُبَ	she may write
2nd dual	تَكْتُبا	you may write
3rd dual (m)	يَكْتُبا	they may write
3rd dual (f)	تَكْتُبا	they may write
1st plural	نَكْتُبَ	we may write
2nd plural (m)	تَكْتُبوا	you may write
2nd plural (f)	تَكْتُبْنَ	you may write
3rd plural (m)	يَكْتُبوا	they may write
3rd plural (f)	يَكْتُبْنَ	they may write

The subjunctive in Arabic is used after a limited range of
conjunctions (*see* **Chapter 14**) to express ideas of purpose, ability
and related concepts. The main conjunctions involved are أَنْ (to)
and لِ (in order to), with its synonyms لِكَيْ ,كَيْ, and لِأَنْ.
أَنْ + subjunctive often provides a convenient way of rendering the
English infinitive. In addition, لَنْ followed by the subjunctive is the
standard way of negating the future. For example:

يريدُ أَنْ يسافرَ إلى اليونان
he wants to travel to Greece

يستطيعُ أَنْ يغادرَ الآن
he can (= is able to) leave now

جئنا لنرى أحمد
we came to (= in order to) see Ahmad

لَنْ تصلَ قبل المساء
she will not arrive before evening

b) Jussive

1st singular	أَكْتُبْ	may I write
2nd singular (m)	تَكْتُبْ	may you write
2nd singular (f)	تَكْتُبي	may you write

3rd singular (m)	يَكْتُبْ	may he write
3rd singular (f)	تَكْتُبْ	may she write
2nd dual	تَكْتُبا	may you write
3rd dual (m)	يَكْتُبا	may they write
3rd dual (f)	تَكْتُبا	may they write
1st plural	نَكْتُبْ	may we write
2nd plural (m)	تَكْتُبوا	may you write
2nd plural (f)	تَكْتُبْنَ	may you write
3rd plural (m)	يَكْتُبوا	may they write
3rd plural (f)	يَكْتُبْنَ	may they write

The jussive may be used either on its own or preceded by لِ to express a wish, or the concept 'may' or 'let'. In modern Arabic, however, it is most commonly found in conjunction with the particle لَمْ to negate the past tense. As such, it is synonymous with ما used in conjunction with the past tense itself – a construction that has become less popular in formal Arabic, partly because it is perceived as colloquial. *See* **Chapter 15** *more on negating the past tense.*

لِيذهب إلى الجحيم!
let him go to hell!

لم أسمع السيارة
I didn't hear the car

لم يسمحوا له بالدخول
they didn't let him come in

 **D. IMPERATIVE**

The imperative is used to give instructions or orders and is formed from the 2nd person forms of the jussive by dropping the prefix تَ.

Since this would result in a word beginning with two consonants, which is impossible in Arabic, a 'helping vowel' is placed at the front of the word.

If the following vowel is a **damma**, as in تَكْتُبْ (may you write), the helping vowel must also be a **damma**. In all other cases the helping vowel is a **kasra**.

2nd singular (m)	اُكْتُبْ	اِرْجِعْ	اِشْرَبْ
2nd singular (f)	اُكْتُبِي	اِرْجِعِي	اِشْرَبِي
2nd dual	اُكْتُبا	اِرْجِعا	اِشْرَبا
2nd plural (m)	اُكْتُبوا	اِرْجِعوا	اِشْرَبوا
2nd plural (f)	اُكْتُبْنَ	اِرْجِعْنَ	اِشْرَبْنَ

E. PASSIVE

The passive form of the simple verb is used when an action is not stated as being performed by a particular person or thing. It is formed by changing the pattern of vowels within the verb. The perfect tense takes the form فُعِل, and the imperfect tense the form يُفْعَل. Passive verbs are conjugated in exactly the same way as active verbs. For example:

ضُرِبْتُمْ
you were beaten

كُتِبَت الرسائل
the letters were written

يُفْهَم
it is understood

سَيُقْتَلون
they will be killed

F. PARTICIPLES AND VERBAL NOUNS

The active participle of the simple verb takes the form فاعِل and the passive participle مَفْعول. Participles change according to case, gender and number in the same way as adjectives. As well as being used in an adjectival sense, many participles are used as nouns, and as such may take broken plurals.

كاتِب
writing/a writer

شارب
drinking

مكتوب
written/a letter

مشروب
a drink

In addition to the active and passive participles, each Arabic verb has an associated verbal noun, which indicates the action or state associated with the verb, and which frequently corresponds in function to the English infinitive. Although the form of the verbal noun in derived form verbs (*see* **Section G**) follows a fixed pattern, simple verb verbal nouns vary in form and should be learned individually. The following examples show some of the variations in form, as well as the usage of the verbal noun. As will be noticed, the verbal noun frequently appears as the first term of an **idāfa** construction.

الكتابة صعبة
writing is difficult

فهم اللغة
the understanding of language

يريدون الذهاب إلى سورية
they want to go (*lit.* going) to Syria

تستطيع دخول الجامعة
she can enter university

G. DERIVED FORMS II–X

The verbs discussed on the previous pages are based on a simple pattern of alternating consonants and vowels in the 3rd person singular of the past tense, eg كتَبَ ,فهمَ, سهُلَ etc. Other verbs are based on more complex patterns, often called 'derived forms', which are numbered II–XV by Western grammarians (though this numbering is seldom used by native speakers of Arabic). Forms

XI-XV, are extremely rare and can be ignored at present. The basic patterns of the remaining forms, using the root ف / ع / ل, are as follows:

(I)	فَعَلَ etc	VI	تَفاعَلَ
II	فَعَّلَ	VII	اِنْفَعَلَ
III	فاعَلَ	VIII	اِفْتَعَلَ
IV	أَفْعَلَ	IX	اِفْعَلَّ
V	تَفَعَّلَ	X	اِسْتَفْعَلَ

The following table shows the forms of the past tense, present tense, active and passive participles and verbal noun of the derived forms II-X:

Form	Past	Present	Active participle	Passive participle	Verbal noun
II	فَعَّلَ	يُفَعِّلُ	مُفَعِّل	مُفَعَّل	التَفْعيل
III	فاعَلَ	يُفاعِلُ	مُفاعِل	مُفاعَل	المُفاعَلة
IV	أَفْعَلَ	يُفْعِلُ	مُفْعِل	مُفْعَل	الإفْعال
V	تَفَعَّلَ	يَتَفَعَّلُ	مُتَفَعِّل	مُتَفَعَّل	التَفَعُّل
VI	تَفاعَلَ	يَتَفاعَلُ	مُتَفاعِل	(مُتَفاعَل)	التَفاعُل
VII	اِنْفَعَلَ	يَنْفَعِلُ	مُنْفَعِل	(مُنْفَعَل)	الاِنْفِعال
VIII	اِفْتَعَلَ	يَفْتَعِلُ	مُفْتَعِل	مُفْتَعَل	الاِفْتِعال
IX	اِفْعَلَّ	يَفْعَلُّ	مُفْعَلّ	مُفْعَلّ	الاِفْعِلال
X	اِسْتَفْعَلَ	يَسْتَفْعِلُ	مُسْتَفْعِل	مُسْتَفْعَل	الاِسْتِفْعال

Note that the forms shown in brackets are seldom used.

H. DOUBLED VERBS

Doubled verbs are verbs in which the second and third root letters are identical. In certain situations, these two root letters are combined and written with a **shadda**. The following table shows the conjugation of a typical doubled verb, مَرَّ (he passed):

	Past	Present Indicative	Subjunctive	Jussive	Imperative
1st sing	مَرَرْتُ	أَمُرُّ	أَمُرَّ	أَمُرَّ	
2nd sing (m)	مَرَرْت	تَمُرُّ	تَمُرَّ	تَمُرَّ	مُرَّ
2nd sing (f)	مَرَرْت	تَمُرِّينَ	تَمُرِّي	تَمُرِّي	مُرِّي
3rd sing (m)	مَرَّ	يَمُرُّ	يَمُرَّ	يَمُرَّ	
3rd sing (f)	مَرَّتْ	تَمُرُّ	تَمُرَّ	تَمُرَّ	
2nd dual	مَرَرْتُما	تَمُرَّانِ	تَمُرَّا	تَمُرَّا	مُرَّا
3rd dual (m)	مَرَّا	يَمُرَّانِ	يَمُرَّا	يَمُرَّا	
3rd dual (f)	مَرَّتا	تَمُرَّانِ	تَمُرَّا	تَمُرَّا	
1st plural	مَرَرْنا	نَمُرُّ	نَمُرَّ	نَمُرَّ	
2nd plural (m)	مَرَرْتُم	تَمُرُّونَ	تَمُرُّوا	تَمُرُّوا	مُرُّوا
2nd plural (f)	مَرَرْتُنَّ	تَمْرُرْنَ	تَمْرُرْنَ	تَمْرُرْنَ	أُمْرُرْنَ
3rd plural (m)	مَرُّوا	يَمُرُّونَ	يَمُرُّوا	يَمُرُّوا	
3rd plural (f)	مَرَرْنَ	يَمْرُرْنَ	يَمْرُرْنَ	يَمْرُرْنَ	

I. WEAK AND HOLLOW VERBS

Weak verbs have و or ي as their final root letter and hollow verbs have و or ي as their middle root letter. Although weak and hollow verbs are sometimes described as 'irregular', this is not the case – rather, their forms change in accordance with certain phonological (sound-related) rules. These rules cause the و or ي to appear as an **alif** (ا) in some situations or to be shortened to a **kasra** or **damma** in others. Although these verbs may seem complicated at first, it is essential to master their basic principles as they include some of the most common words in the Arabic language, eg كان (to be), قال (to say) etc.

The following tables show examples of the main types of weak and hollow verbs.

1 Verbs with و as their middle radical, for example قالَ (to say), root ق / و / ل

	Past	Present Indicative	Subjunctive	Jussive	Imperative
1st sing	قُلْتُ	أقولُ	أقولَ	أقُلْ	
2nd sing (m)	قُلْتَ	تقولُ	تقولَ	تقُلْ	قُلْ
2nd sing (f)	قُلْتِ	تقولينَ	تقولي	تقولي	قولي
3rd sing (m)	قالَ	يقولُ	يقولَ	يقُلْ	
3rd sing (f)	قالَتْ	تقولُ	تقولَ	تقُلْ	
2nd dual	قُلْتُما	تَقولانِ	تَقولا	تَقولا	قولا
3rd dual (m)	قالا	يَقولانِ	يَقولا	يَقولا	
3rd dual (f)	قالَتا	تَقولانِ	تَقولا	تَقولا	
1st plural	قُلْنا	نَقولُ	نَقولَ	نَقُلْ	
2nd plural (m)	قُلْتُم	تقولونَ	تقولوا	تقولوا	قولوا
2nd plural (f)	قُلْتُنَّ	تَقُلْنَ	تَقُلْنَ	تَقُلْنَ	قُلْنَ
3rd plural (m)	قالوا	يَقولونَ	يَقولوا	يَقولوا	
3rd plural (f)	قُلْنَ	يَقُلْنَ	يَقُلْنَ	يَقُلْنَ	

2 Verbs with ي as their middle radical, for example سارَ (to walk), root س / ي / ر

	Past	Present Indicative	Subjunctive	Jussive	Imperative
1st sing	سِرْتُ	أسيرُ	أسيرَ	أسِرْ	
2nd sing (m)	سِرْتَ	تَسيرُ	تَسيرَ	تَسِرْ	سِرْ
2nd sing (f)	سِرْتِ	تَسيرينَ	تَسيري	تَسيري	سيري
3rd sing (m)	سارَ	يَسيرُ	يَسيرَ	يَسِرْ	

	Past	Present Indicative	Subjunctive	Jussive	Imperative
3rd sing (f)	سارَت	تَسيرُ	تَسيرَ	تَسِر	
2nd dual	سِرتُما	تَسيران	تَسيرا	تَسيرا	سيرا
3rd dual (m)	سارَا	يَسيران	يَسيرا	يَسيرا	
3rd dual (f)	سارَتا	تَسيران	تَسيرا	تَسيرا	
1st plural	سِرنا	نَسيرُ	نَسيرَ	نَسِر	
2nd plural (m)	سِرتُم	تَسيرون	تَسيروا	تَسيروا	سيروا
2nd plural (f)	سِرتُنَّ	تَسِرنَ	تَسِرنَ	تَسِرنَ	سِرنَ
3rd plural (m)	ساروا	يَسيرون	يَسيروا	يَسيروا	
3rd plural (f)	سِرنَ	يَسِرنَ	يَسِرنَ	يَسِرنَ	

3 Verbs with و or ي as their middle radical, and a **kasra** as the middle vowel in the perfect tense, for example خاف (to fear), root خ / ي / ف

	Past	Present Indicative	Subjunctive	Jussive	Imperative
1st sing	خِفت	أخافُ	أخافَ	أخَف	
2nd sing (m)	خِفت	تَخافُ	تَخافَ	تَخَف	خَف
2nd sing (f)	خِفت	تَخافينَ	تَخافي	تَخافي	خافي
3rd sing (m)	خافَ	يَخافُ	يَخافَ	يَخَف	
3rd sing (f)	خافَت	تَخافُ	تَخافَ	تَخَف	
2nd dual	خِفتُما	تَخافان	تَخافا	تَخافا	خافا
3rd dual (m)	خافا	يَخافان	يَخافا	يَخافا	
3rd dual (f)	خافتا	تَخافان	تَخافا	تَخافا	
1st plural	خِفنا	نَخافُ	نَخافَ	نَخَف	
2nd plural (m)	خِفتُم	تَخافونَ	تَخافوا	تَخافوا	خافوا
2nd plural (f)	خِفتُنَّ	تَخَفنَ	تَخَفنَ	تَخَفنَ	خَفنَ
3rd plural (m)	خافوا	يَخافونَ	يَخافوا	يَخافوا	
3rd plural (f)	خِفنَ	يَخَفنَ	يَخَفنَ	يَخَفنَ	

4 Verbs with a ي as the final radical, for example بَنَى (to build), root ب / ن / ي

	Past	Present			
		Indicative	Subjunctive	Jussive	Imperative
1st sing	بَنَيْتُ	أَبْنِي	أَبْنِيَ	أَبْنِ	
2nd sing *(m)*	بَنَيْتَ	تَبْنِي	تَبْنِيَ	تَبْنِ	اِبْنِ
2nd sing *(f)*	بَنَيْتِ	تَبْنِينَ	تَبْنِي	تَبْنِي	اِبْنِي
3rd sing *(m)*	بَنَى	يَبْنِي	يَبْنِيَ	يَبْنِ	
3rd sing *(f)*	بَنَت	تَبْنِي	تَبْنِيَ	تَبْنِ	
2nd dual	بَنَيْتُما	تَبْنِيانِ	تَبْنِيا	تَبْنِيا	اِبْنِيا
3rd dual *(m)*	بَنَيا	يَبْنِيانِ	يَبْنِيا	يَبْنِيا	
3rd dual *(f)*	بَنَتا	تَبْنِيانِ	تَبْنِيا	تَبْنِيا	
1st plural	بَنَيْنا	نَبْنِي	نَبْنِيَ	نَبْنِ	
2nd plural *(m)*	بَنَيْتُم	تَبْنُونَ	تَبْنُوا	تَبْنُوا	اِبْنوا
2nd plural *(f)*	بَنَيْتُنَّ	تَبْنِينَ	تَبْنِينَ	تَبْنِينَ	اِبْنينَ
3rd plural *(m)*	بَنَوْنَ	يَبْنُونَ	يَبْنُوا	يَبْنُوا	
3rd plural *(f)*	بَنَيْنَ	يَبْنِينَ	يَبْنِينَ	يَبْنِينَ	

5 Verbs with a و as the final radical, for example دَعا (to invite), root د / ع / و

	Past	Present			
		Indicative	Subjunctive	Jussive	Imperative
1st sing	دَعَوْتُ	أَدعو	أَدعو	أَدْعُ	
2nd sing *(m)*	دَعَوْتَ	تَدعو	تَدعو	تَدْعُ	اُدْعُ
2nd sing *(f)*	دَعَوْتِ	تَدعين	تَدعي	تَدْعي	اُدْعي
3rd sing *(m)*	دَعا	يَدْعو	يَدعو	يَدْعُ	
3rd sing *(f)*	دَعَت	تَدعو	تَدعو	تَدْعُ	
2nd dual	دَعَوْتُما	تَدْعُوانِ	تَدْعُوا	تَدْعُوا	اُدْعُوا

	Past	Present Indicative	Subjunctive	Jussive	Imperative
3rd dual (m)	دَعَوا	يَدْعُوان	يَدْعُوا	يَدْعُوا	
3rd dual (f)	دَعَتا	تَدْعُوان	تَدْعُوا	تَدْعُوا	
1st plural	دَعَوْنا	نَدْعو	نَدْعُوَ	نَدْعُ	
2nd plural (m)	دَعَوْتُمْ	تَدْعون	تَدْعوا	تَدْعوا	أُدْعوا
2nd plural (f)	دَعَوْتُنَّ	تَدْعون	تَدْعونَ	تَدْعونَ	أُدْعونَ
3rd plural (m)	دَعَوْا	يَدْعون	يَدْعوا	يَدْعوا	
3rd plural (f)	دَعَوْنَ	يَدْعون	يَدْعونَ	يَدْعونَ	

6 Verbs with a ي or و as the final radical and a **kasra** as the middle vowel in the perfect tense, for example نَسِيَ (to forget), root ن / س / ي

	Past	Present Indicative	Subjunctive	Jussive	Imperative
1st sing	نَسيتُ	أَنْسى	أَنْسى	أَنْسَ	
2nd sing (m)	نَسيت	تَنْسى	تَنْسى	تَنْسَ	انْسَ
2nd sing (f)	نَسيت	تَنْسينَ	تَنْسَيْ	تَنْسَيْ	انْسَيْ
3rd sing (m)	نَسِيَ	يَنْسى	يَنْسى	يَنْسَ	
3rd sing (f)	نَسيت	تَنْسى	تَنْسى	تَنْسَ	
2nd dual	نَسيتُما	تَنْسيان	تَنْسَيا	تَنْسَيا	انْسَيا
3rd dual (m)	نَسِيا	يَنْسيان	يَنْسَيا	يَنْسَيا	
3rd dual (f)	نَسِيَتا	تَنْسيان	تَنْسَيا	تَنْسَيا	
1st plural	نَسينا	نَنْسى	نَنْسى	نَنْسَ	
2nd plural (m)	نَسيتُم	تَنْسونَ	تَنْسَوا	تَنْسَوا	انْسَوا
2nd plural (f)	نَسيتُنَّ	تَنْسَيْنَ	تَنْسَيْنَ	تَنْسَيْنَ	انْسَيْنَ
3rd plural (m)	نَسوا	يَنْسونَ	يَنْسَوا	يَنْسَوا	
3rd plural (f)	نَسِينَ	يَنْسَيْنَ	يَنْسَيْنَ	يَنْسَيْنَ	

J. THE VERBS 'TO BE' (كان) AND 'NOT TO BE' (ليس)

The verb كان (to be) in Arabic is a hollow verb of type 1 (*see*
Section I), which is conjugated in the same way as قال (to say):

	Past	Present Indicative	Subjunctive	Jussive	Imperative
1st sing	كُنْتُ	أكونُ	أكونَ	أكُنْ	
2nd sing *(m)*	كُنْتَ	تكونُ	تكونَ	تكُنْ	كُنْ
2nd sing *(f)*	كُنْتِ	تكونينَ	تكوني	تكوني	كوني
3rd sing *(m)*	كانَ	يكونُ	يكونَ	يكُنْ	
3rd sing *(f)*	كانتْ	تكونُ	تكونَ	تكُنْ	

etc

In all tenses except for the present indicative, كان functions in the
same way as any other verb. Note, however, that unlike in most
European languages, the complement of the verb must be in the
accusative rather than the nominative case:

كان طالباً	ستكون سعيدةً جداً
he was a student	she will be very happy
لم أكُنْ في البيت	لنْ نكونَ موجودين
I wasn't in the house	we won't be present

In the present tense, no verb is usually used to express the concept
of 'to be' (equivalent to the English 'am', 'is', 'are' *etc*):

هل أنت في نفس الغرفة؟	هؤلاء الطلّاب سوريون
are you in the same room?	these students are Syrian
هذه الكتب غالية جداً	
these books are very expensive	

To express the negative of the verb 'to be' in the present tense,
Arabic uses a special verb ليسَ (not to be), which is conjugated as

follows (note that the verb is present in meaning although it uses perfect tense suffixes):

1st sing	لَسْتُ	I am not
2nd sing (m)	لَسْتَ	you are not
2nd sing (f)	لَسْتِ	you are not
3rd sing (m)	لَيْسَ	he is not/it is not
3rd sing (f)	لَيْسَتْ	she is not/they are not
2nd dual	لَسْتُما	you are not
1st plural	لَسْنا	we are not
2nd plural (m)	لَسْتُمْ	you are not
2nd plural (f)	لَسْتُنَّ	you are not
3rd plural (m)	لَيْسوا	they are not
3rd plural (f)	لَسْنَ	they are not

Note that the predicate (the word describing the subject), like the predicate of كان, is in the accusative:

ليس الطالب ذكياً جداً
the student is not very intelligent

لستُ مصرياً
I am not Egyptian

ليست هذه الكتب جديدةً
these books are not new

K. COMPOUND TENSES

In addition to its function as the equivalent of the verb 'to be', the verb كان is also used in conjunction with other verbs to form compound tenses, including (most commonly) a 'continuous past' or 'repeated past' tense ('he was going, he used to go' *etc*), and the equivalent of the English pluperfect ('he had gone' *etc*). Other combinations may also occasionally be found, for example the equivalent of the future perfect (he will have gone).

كان يجلس في غرفته
he was sitting in his room

كانت المدرّسة تشرب الشاي
the teacher (f) used to drink tea

كنت (قد) كتبت الرسالة
I had written the letter

كانوا (قد) ذهبوا الى المدرسة
they had gone to school

ستكون قد نجحت
you will have succeeded

L. 'IRREGULAR' VERBS

As we have seen, Arabic has very few genuinely irregular verbs.
In addition to ليس ('not to be'; *see* Section J), the verb رأى (to see)
should be noted, as it loses the **hamza** in the present tense:

	Past	Present			
		Indicative	*Subjunctive*	*Jussive*	*Imperative*
1st sing	رَأَيْتُ	أَرى	أَرى	أَرَ	
2nd sing (m)	رَأَيْتَ	تَرى	تَرى	تَرَ	(رَ)
2nd sing (f)	رَأَيْتِ	تَرَيْنَ	تَرَيْ	تَرَيْ	(رَيْ)
3rd sing (m)	رَأى	يَرى	يَرى	يَرَ	
3rd sing (f)	رَأَتْ	تَرى	تَرى	تَرَ	

etc

Note that the imperative forms of this verb are in practice never
used.

14 CONJUNCTIONS

Conjunctions are words that are used to link and explain the relationship between two clauses.

1 وَ (and)

The single letter وَ is by far the most common conjunction in Arabic, and can usually be translated simply as 'and'. It is always written as part of the word it precedes, rather than as a separate word.

جاء عمّار ونادر إلى المحاضرة
Ammar and Nader came to the lecture

أدرّس في الجامعة يوم الخميس ويوم الجمعة
I teach in the university on Thursdays and Fridays

Whereas in English the word 'and' is generally only used between the final two items in a list, Arabic uses وَ between all items in a list:

السنة الماضية زارت وجدان تركيا وجورجيا وروسيا واليونان
(*lit.* last year, Wijdan visited Turkey and Georgia and Russia and Greece)
last year, Wijdan visited Turkey, Georgia, Russia and Greece

ذهبتُ إلى السوق واشتريتُ كتاباً وجريدةً وقميصاً وسجائر
(*lit.* I went to the market and bought a book and a newspaper and a shirt and some cigarettes)
I went to the market and bought a book, a newspaper, a shirt and some cigarettes

2 فَ (then, so)

The single letter conjunction فَ attaches to the following word and has a range of meanings.

a) 'Then'

When two events occur in sequence, فَ is used to mean 'then'. In this sense, it may be used to link both verbs and nouns:

دخل أحمد فخالد الغرفة

Ahmed entered the room, then Khalid

أَكلتُ تفاحاً فشربت قهوة

I ate an apple then drank some coffee

b) 'So'

فَ is commonly used to link two clauses where the second clause is a direct consequence of the first:

لم أستطع النوم فقرأتُ قليلاً

I couldn't sleep, so I read a little

فشل سيف الدين في امتحاناته فلم يدخل الجامعة

Seyf ad-Din failed his exams, so he didn't go to university

b) 'As', 'since', 'for'

فَ may also be used to introduce a clause and provide an explanation for something that happened in the past:

لم تنجح هدى في المدرسة فقد كانت مريضةً

Hoda wasn't successful at school as she'd been ill

3 ثُمَّ **(then)**

The conjunction ثُمَّ is used to put events in order:

شرب لوُي القهوة ثمَّ ذهب إلى السينما

Loai drank coffee then went to the cinema

درست تهاني اللغة الإنجليزية في الجامعة ثمَّ أصبحت أستاذة

Tahani studied English at university, then she became a teacher

4 أوْ **(or)**

The conjunction أوْ is used in almost exactly the same way as 'or' in English:

يمكنني أن أذهب إلى أمريكا أو كندا لأحضِر الماجستير

I can go to either America or Australia to do my Masters

في الصباح تشرب القهوة أو الشاي

in the morning she drinks coffee or tea

However, if a question is formed using 'or', then أَم is used instead:

هل تحبّني أم لا؟	هل أنت من الجزائر أم وهران؟
do you love me or not?	are you from Algiers or Oran?

5 لكنَّ and لكنْ (but)

لكنَّ and لكنْ are used in the same way as 'but' in English. They are often preceded by the conjunction وَ. In general, لكنَّ is used before nouns, while لكنْ is used before verbs or other parts of speech:

في مدينة كسلا مقاه عديدة ولكن ليس فيها سينما

Kassala has many cafes but there's no cinema

هيثم يحب القهوة ولكنَّ حسن يفضل الشاي

Haitham likes coffee but Hassan prefers tea

Pronoun suffixes can also be added to لكنَّ:

غبت في الالتحاق بكلية الطب ولكنني لم أنجح

I wanted to go to the Faculty of Medicine, but didn't succeed

كنت أنتظر مها ولكنَّها ما جاءت

I was waiting for Maha but she didn't come

See also **Chapter 17, Section A.**

6 كذلك (as well, as well as)

عنده ثلاثة دكاكين وبيتان وكذلك سيارة

he has three shops, two houses and a car as well

كلّنا نذهب إلى السوق: أحمد وفيصل وأنا كذالك

we're all going to the market; Ahmed and Faisal as well as me

7 مع أنّ (even though)

كانت السماء تمطر مع أنّ الشمس مشرقة
it was raining even though the sun was shining

حصلت منى على تقدير ممتاز في اللغة العربية مع أنها لغة صعبة
Muna got an excellent result in Arabic even though it's a difficult language

8 أما (as for)

أما is used to introduce a change of subject noun or pronoun ('as for me', 'as for the French' etc). The conjunction فـ is used to introduce the following predicate:

يدرس أخي الكيمياء أما أنا فأدرس التاريخ
my brother studies chemistry, as for me, I study history

دمشق مدينة آمنة. أما بغداد فإنها مدينة خطيرة جداً
Damascus is a safe city. As for Baghdad, well it's a very dangerous city

9 إما (either ... or)

إما is used in constructions of choice and can be translated as 'either ... or' in English. The first choice is introduced by إما, while the second choice is introduced by either وإما or أو:

اليوم سأذاكر إما اللغة العربية أو اللغة الفارسية
today I will revise either Arabic or Persian

لا أعرف إلى أين سأسافر السنة القادمة. إما موريتانيا وإما الجزائر
I don't know where I'll travel next year. Either Mauritania or Algeria

15 NEGATIVE AND INTERROGATIVE PARTICLES

A. NEGATIVE PARTICLES

1 Uses of لا

a) Negating the present tense

To negate a simple verb in the present tense, لا (not) precedes the verb:

لا نستطيعُ المجيءَ إلى النادي اليوم
we can't come to the club today

لا أحبُّ أن أشربَ الشاي بالحليب
I don't like to drink tea with milk

لا يعملُ فيصل في الأمم المتحدة
Faisal doesn't work at the United Nations

لا توجد فنادق كثيرة في مدينة جوبا
there aren't many hotels in the city of Juba

See also **Chapter 13, Section B** *for more on simple verbs.*

b) Negating the imperative

For a negative command, لا is used before the jussive form of the verb:

لا تدخنْ داخل البيت، من فضلك
don't smoke inside the house, please

لا تأتِ إلى المحاضرة متأخراً
don't come late to the lecture

يا ماجدة، لا تجلسي على الكرسي المكسور
Magda, don't sit on the broken chair

لا تذهبوا إلى بغداد، إنها خطيرة حالياً
don't go to Baghdad, as it's dangerous at the moment

See also **Chapter 13, Section D.**

c) 'Nobody/no-one'

لا can also be used with أحَد (one) to mean 'nobody', 'no-one' or 'none of':

لا أحَدَ قادرٌ على المجيء اليوم   لا أحَدَ من أصدقائي موريتانيٌّ
nobody is able to come today   none of my friends is Mauritanian

d) 'Neither ... nor ...'

The construction لا ...ولا... can be used to express 'neither ... nor ...':

ما ساعدني أحد ، لا عبد الله ولا أكرم
nobody helped me, neither Abdullah nor Akram

لا أريد أن أشرب شيئاً، لا القهوة ولا الشاي
I don't want anything to drink, neither coffee nor tea

2 Uses of لن

لن (not) is used to negate the future tense. The verb that follows it is in the subjunctive:

لن يسافرَ الزين إلى جبوتي السنة القادمة
Zain will not travel to Djibouti next year

لن نستطيعَ دخول مكتبة الجامعة خلال الإجازة
we won't be able to enter the university library during the holiday

الموضوع مقفول ولن نتحدثَ عنه مرة أخرى
the subject is closed and we won't discuss it again

لن تجدَ أرخص من تلك الأسعار في مكان آخر
you won't find prices cheaper than these elsewhere

See also **Chapter 13, Section C.**

3 Uses of لم

لم (not) is used with the jussive form of the present tense verb to negate the past tense:

لم يدرسْ محمود جيداً للامتحان
Mahmoud didn't study well for his exam

لم نأكل الفطور فأصبحنا جوعانين الآن
we didn't have breakfast so we're hungry now

لم أستطع الحصول على تأشيرة لزيارة ليبيا
I couldn't get a visa to visit Libya

لم يعرف علي اللغة الإنجليزية قبل سفره إلى لندن
Ali didn't know English before he travelled to London

See also **Chapter 13, Section C.**

4 Uses of ليْسَ

a) Negating كان (to be)

Nominal sentences (*see* **Chapter 17, Section A**) with the verb كان (to be) in the present tense are negated using the forms of the verb ليْسَ, as set out in **Chapter 13, Section J**:

لَسْتُ مصريا	ليْسَتْ نسرين أستاذةً
I'm not Egyptian	Nasreen isn't a teacher
لسْتُم طلاباً جيدين	ليْسَتْ تلك البنتُ متزوجةً
you're not good students (*m*)	that girl isn't married
ليْسَ الولدُ ذكياً	ليْسَ الجو بارداً في السودان
the boy isn't clever	the weather isn't cold in Sudan
ليْسَت جورجيا بلداً عربياً	
Georgia isn't an Arab country	

لي أصدقاء كثيرون ولكن ليْسوا موجودين اليوم
I have many friends but they're not here today (*m*)

b) With a possessive construction

The third person singular forms of the verb ليْسَ (لَيْسَ and لَيْسَتْ)

can be used to negate possessive constructions:

لَيْسَ لي أخ

I don't have a brother

عبد الرحيم لَيْسَ (ليست) عنده سيارة

Abdulrahim doesn't have a car

هدى لَيْسَ معها فلوس

Huda does not have any money with her

لَيْسَ في مدينة سواكن جامعة

there isn't a university in Suakin

See also **Chapter 9, Section B** *for more information on negating possessives.*

5 Uses of ما

a) Negating كان (to be) in the past tense:

في طفولتي ما كنتُ آكل اللحم

in my childhood I didn't use to eat meat

ما كان عندنا وقت

we didn't have time

ذهبنا إلى المتحف ولكنّه ما كان مفتوحاً

we went to the museum but it wasn't open

See also **Chapter 13, Section J.**

b) Informal use

ما is a more informal alternative to both لم (used to negate the past tense) and لَيْسَ (used to negate possessive constructions).

  i) When it precedes the past tense form of the verb, ما can be used to negate the past tense:

Formal

لم أدرس اللغة الإسبانية في المدرسة

I didn't study Spanish at school

لم نشرب البيرة قبل الذهاب إلى السينما

we didn't drink beer before going to the cinema

Informal

مـا درستُ اللغة الإسبانية في المدرسة

I didn't study Spanish at school

مـا شربنا البيرة قبل الذهاب إلى السينما

we didn't drink beer before going to the cinema

See also **Chapter 13, Section B.**

ii) مـا can be used in place of ليْسَ to negate some possessive
   constructions:

Formal

نادر ليس له أخت

Nader doesn't have a sister

هل معك قلم؟ لا، ليس معي

do you have a pen? No, I don't have one

ليس عندنا بيتٌ كبيرٌ

we don't have a large house

Informal

نادر مـا له أخت

Nader doesn't have a sister

هل معك قلم؟ لا، مـا معي

do you have a pen? No, I don't have one

مـا عندنا بيتٌ كبيرٌ

we don't have a large house

See also **Chapter 9, Section B.**

B. INTERROGATIVE PARTICLES

These are used to form question words.

1 Yes/no questions

The word هل is used at the start of a sentence to form a yes/no question. For example:

هل تعرف عاصمة إيران؟
do you know the capital of Iran?

هل أنت مغربي؟
are you Moroccan?

هل هذا الرجل مهندس؟
is this man an engineer?

هل يدرس أحمد الطب؟
does Ahmed study medicine?

هل سمعت آخر الأخبار من اليمن؟
have you heard the latest news from Yemen?

هل ستحتفل بعيد الأضحى مع عائلتك؟
will you celebrate Eid al-Adha with your family?

If the yes/no question is negative, (eg 'don't you?', 'isn't it?' *etc*), then the single letter أ is used with the appropriate negative particle to form the question. *See* **Section A.**

أليس عندك وقت؟
don't you have time?

ألم تزُر مصر من قبل؟
haven't you visited Egypt before?

ألا تعرف أسماء كل الطلاب؟
don't you know the names of all the students?

ألن تسافر إلى أمريكا هذا الصيف؟
won't you be travelling to America this summer?

2 Question words

a) ماذا and ما (what)

ماذا meaning 'what?' is always followed by a verb:

ماذا يعمل أبوك؟
what does your father do?

ماذا تدرس في الجامعة؟
what do you study at university?

عندما ذهبت إلى السودان، ماذا أكلت؟
when you went to Sudan, what did you eat?

ماذا يتكلم الناس في الصومال؟
what do people in Somalia speak?

ما is used to form questions such as 'what is/are ...?':

ما هو كتابك المفضل؟
what's your favourite book?

ما اسمك؟
what's your name?

ما رأيك؟
what's your opinion?

ما هي الأشياء التي تحتاج إليها للسفر إلى الخارج؟
what are the things you need to travel abroad?

Prepositions can also be added before ما to form the following types of question:

عَمَّ = عن + ما	لِمَ = لـ + ما	بِمَ = بـ + ما
about what?	(*lit.* for what?) why?	with what?

b) لماذا (why)

لَماذا meaning 'why?' is more commonly used than لِمَ (for what, why?):

لماذا تدرس اللغة العربية؟
why are you studying Arabic?

لِمَ بُنِيَ سدّ أسوان؟
why was the Aswan Dam built?

لماذا كسرت الشباك يا غبي؟!
stupid boy, why did you break the window?!

لماذا بدأت الحرب بين روسيا وجورجيا؟
why did the war between Russia and Georgia start?

c) مَتى (when)

متى ستغادر غداً؟
when are you leaving tomorrow?

متى تبدأ المحاضرة؟
when does the lecture begin?

متى وُلِدَت الملكة بلقيس؟
when was Cleopatra, Queen of Sheba born?

متى تحب أن تدرس؟ في الصباح أم في المساء؟
when do you like to study? In the morning or in the evening?

d) كَيْفَ (how)

كيف تقول «كتاب» باللغة الإنجليزية؟
how do you say كتاب in English?

كيف حالكم اليوم؟
how are you today?

كيف سنذهب إلى السعودية بدون تأشيرة؟
how can we go to Saudi Arabia without a visa?

كيف تعرفت على زوجتك، يا كاظم؟
how did you meet your wife, Kazem?

e) أَيْنَ (where)

أين يتكلمون اللغة الأرمنية؟
where do they speak Armenian?

أين يسكن عادل؟
where does 'Aadil live?

إلى أين تذهبين، يا سوسن؟
where are you going, Sawsan?

من أين جاء ذلك الكلب؟
where did that dog come from?

f) مَن (who)

من درّسك اللغة العربية؟
who taught you Arabic?

من هو بشار الأسد؟
who is Bashar al-Assad?

مع من ذهبت إلى بيروت؟
who did you go to Beirut with?

لمن تشتري هدايا في عيد الميلاد؟
at Christmas, who do you buy presents for?

g) كَم (how many)
The question word كَم (how many) is almost always followed by an indefinite noun in the singular. This noun takes the accusative case.

كم أخاً وأختاً لك؟

how many brothers and sisters do you have?

كم بلداً زرته في حياتك؟

how many countries have you visited in your life?

لا أعرف كم مرة أنا طلبت منه المساعدة ؟!

I asked him for help I don't know how many times!

كم ديناراً يساوي جنيهاً إسترلينياً واحداً؟

how many dinars to the pound?

The preposition بـ can be added to كم in order to form the
question بِكَم؟ (how much?):

بكم هذا الكتاب؟

how much is this book?

سيارتك الجديدة جميلة. بكم اشتريتها؟

your new car is beautiful. How much did you pay for it?

h) أيّ (which)

The question word أيّ (which) always appears before the noun:

في أيّ مدينة يسكن هشام؟   أيّ فيلم تريد أن تشاهد؟

in which city does Hisham live?   which film do you want to watch?

Object pronoun suffixes can be added to أيّ to form a question
beginning with 'which one?':

القضارف وواد مدني مدينتان سودانيتان. في رأيك، أيّهما الأجمل؟

Gedarif and Wad Medani are Sudanese cities. In your opinion, which
one is the most beautiful?

16 NUMBERS, DATES AND TIME

A. CARDINAL NUMBERS

For the Arabic numerals, see **Chapter 1, Section E.**

Cardinal numbers are the standard number forms, eg 'one', 'ten', 'forty', as opposed to ordinal numbers, eg 'first', 'second'.

1 Forms

	Masculine	*Feminine*
1	واحِد/ أَحَد	واحِدة/ إِحْدى
2	اثنان	اثنتان
3	ثلاثة	ثلاث
4	أَرْبَعة	أَرْبَع
5	خَمْسة	خَمْس
6	سِتَّة	سِتّ
7	سَبْعة	سَبْع
8	ثَمانِية	ثَمان
9	تِسْعة	تِسْع
10	عَشَرة	عَشْر
11	أَحَد عَشَر	إِحْدى عَشْرة
12	اثنا عَشَر	اثنتا عَشْرة
13	ثَلاثة عَشَر	ثَلاث عَشْرة
14	أَرْبَعة عَشَر	أَرْبَع عَشْرة
15	خَمْسة عَشَر	خَمْس عَشْرة
16	سِتَّة عَشَر	سِتّ عَشْرة
17	سَبْعة عَشَر	سَبْع عَشْرة

	Masculine	*Feminine*
18	ثمانِيَةَ عَشَرَ	ثمانِيَ عَشْرَةَ
19	تِسْعَةَ عَشَرَ	تِسْعَ عَشْرَةَ
20	عِشْرونَ	عِشْرونَ
21	أَحَدٌ وَعِشْرونَ	إحْدَى وَعِشْرونَ
22	اثنان وَعِشْرونَ	ثِنْتان وَعِشْرونَ
23	ثَلاثَةٌ وَعِشْرونَ	ثَلاثٌ وَعِشْرونَ
24	أَرْبَعَةٌ وَعِشْرونَ	أَرْبَعٌ وَعِشْرونَ
25	خَمْسَةٌ وَعِشْرونَ	خَمْسٌ وَعِشْرونَ
26	سِتَّةٌ وَعِشْرونَ	سِتٌّ وَعِشْرونَ
27	سَبْعَةٌ وَعِشْرونَ	سَبْعٌ وَعِشْرونَ
28	ثمانِيَةٌ وَعِشْرونَ	ثمانٍ وَعِشْرونَ
29	تِسْعَةٌ وَعِشْرونَ	تِسْعٌ وَعِشْرونَ
30	ثَلاثونَ	ثَلاثونَ
31	أَحَدٌ وَثَلاثونَ	إحْدَى وَثَلاثونَ
32	اثنان وَثَلاثونَ	ثِنْتان وَثَلاثونَ
40	أَرْبَعونَ	أَرْبَعونَ
41	أَحَدٌ وَأَرْبَعونَ	إحْدَى وَأَرْبَعونَ
50	خَمْسونَ	خَمْسونَ
60	سِتّونَ	سِتّونَ
70	سَبْعونَ	سَبْعونَ
80	ثمانونَ	ثمانونَ
90	تِسْعونَ	تِسْعونَ
100	مِئة (مائة)	مِئة (مائة)
101	مِئة وَواحِد	مِئة وَواحِدة
102	مِئة وَاثْنان	مِئة وَاثْنتان

	Masculine	*Feminine*
110	مئة وَعشَرَة	مئة وَعشَر
111	مئة وَإحَد عَشَر	مئة وَإحْدى عَشْرَة
112	مئة وَاثنا عَشَر	مئة وَاثنَتا عَشْرَة
120	مئة وَعشرون	مئة وَعشرون
121	مئة وَأحَد وَعشرون	مئة وَإحْدى وعشرون
122	مئة وَاثنان وَعشرون	مئة وَاثْنَتان وعشرون
130	مئة وَثلاثون	مئة وَثلاثون
140	مئة وَأربَعون	مئة وَأربَعون
150	مئة وَخمْسون	مئة وَخمْسون
200	مئتان	مئتان
201	مئتان وواحد	مئتان وواحدة
202	مئتان واثنان	مئتان واثنتان
300	ثلاث مئة، ثَلاثمئة	ثلاث مئة، ثَلاثمئة
400	أربع مئة	أربع مئة
500	خمْس مئة	خمْس مئة
600	ست مئة	ست مئة
700	سَبْع مئة	سَبْع مئة
800	ثماني مئة	ثماني مئة
900	تسْع مئة	تسْع مئة
1,000	ألف	ألف
2,000	ألفان	ألفان
3,000	ثلاثة آلاف	ثلاثة آلاف
4,000	أربعة آلاف	أربعة آلاف
5,000	خمْسة آلاف	خمْسة آلاف
10,000	عشَرة آلاف	عشَرة آلاف
100,000	مئة ألف	مئة ألف

	Masculine	*Feminine*
200,000	مِئَتا أَلْف	مِئَتا أَلْف
1,000,000	مَلْيون	مَلْيون
2,000,000	مَلْيونان	مَلْيونان
3,000,000	ثَلاثَة مَلايين	ثَلاثَة مَلايين

Note that the numbers 400 to 900 may also be written as one word.

2 Usage

Arabic numbers represent one of the biggest obstacles for the foreign learner, as the system is extremely complex. In spoken Arabic the numbers system has been simplified, but the basic principles (eg the use of singular and plural nouns) have generally been retained. These are explained below.

a) The two words for 'one', أَحَد / إحدى and واحد / واحدة are not generally interchangeable.

   i) واحد *(m)* and واحدة *(f)* are used in counting, and as an adjective following the noun:

      قلم واحد
      one pen

      مدينة واحدة
      one city

   These phrases emphasize the number. It is not necessary to use واحد or واحدة in phrases such as 'a pen', 'a city' *etc*.

   ii) أَحَد *(m)* and إحدى *(f)* appear in some compound numbers and in **idāfa** constructions, meaning 'one of'. Note that إحدى *(f)* becomes إحدا if a pronoun suffix is added:

      أحد الكتب
      one of the books
      إحدى الطالبات مصرية وإحداهنّ ليبية
      one of the students *(f)* is Egyptian, and one of them *(f)* is Libyan

أَحد is also used to mean 'anyone' or 'no-one' in sentences such as the following:

لا أحد هنا!

there's no-one here!

هل هناك أحد في الغرفة؟

is there anyone in the room?

لم أر أحداً في المكتبة

I didn't see anyone in the library

b) The word for 'two' اثنان / اثنتان is used in counting and as an adjective following the noun:

بيتان اثنان

two houses

اشترى سيّارتين اثنتين

he bought two cars

Since the dual ending alone conveys the idea of 'two' (eg بيتان 'two houses' *see* **Chapter 4, Section D**), this sort of phrase is quite uncommon. However, it can be used to emphasize or contrast.

c) The numbers 'three' to 'ten' are followed by an indefinite noun in the genitive plural. The ending of the number must agree in case. Note that the form of the number with the feminine marker **tā` marbūta** is used with masculine nouns, and vice versa:

ثلاثة أبواب

three doors

خمس مدن

five cities

ستّ أساتذة وثماني طالبات

six professors and eight students *(f)*

See **Chapter 6** *for more on case endings.*

d) The numbers from 11 to 19 are particularly complex, but their rules have been greatly simplified in spoken Arabic. They are followed by an indefinite noun in the accusative case. Note that these numbers do not vary according to gender, number or case:

خَمْسَةَ عَشَرَ كتاباً

fifteen books

أَرْبَعَ عَشْرَةَ قريةً

fourteen villages

e) For the numbers 20 to 99, the tens behave as sound masculine plural nouns and change when in the accusative or genitive case (eg عشرون 'twenty' becomes عشرين):

رأيت عشرين بيتاً
I saw twenty houses

في سبع وثلاثين مدرسةً
in thirty-seven schools

f) The numbers مئة (hundred), ألف (thousand), مليون (million) and their compounds are followed by a noun in the genitive singular:

مئة كلب
100 dogs

ثلاثة آلاف سنة
3,000 years

ألف ليلة وليلة
(*lit.* a thousand nights and a night) 1,001 nights

g) When forming compound numbers in modern Arabic, the order is thousands, hundreds, units, tens. Each element is connected to the next with و, except within the numbers 11 to 19.
If the compound number is followed by a noun, the noun will take its number and case from the last element in the number. For example:

في مئة وثلاث وعشرين دولةً
in 123 states

ألفان وخمس مئة وستة دنانير
2,506 dinars

h) Phrases that include a number and the definite article (eg 'the six men') are usually formed by placing the definite article and number after the noun. The number must agree with the noun in gender:

النساء السبع
the seven women

أولاد المدرّس الثلاثة
the teacher's three children

B. ORDINAL NUMBERS

Ordinal numbers are used to express order, eg 'first', 'second', 'third', 'fourth' *etc.*

1 Forms

	Masculine	Feminine
1st	الأوَّل	الأولى
2nd	الثاني	الثانية
3rd	الثالث	الثالثة
4th	الرابع	الرابعة
5th	الخامس	الخامسة
6th	السادس	السادسة
7th	السابع	السابعة
8th	الثامن	الثامنة
9th	التاسع	التاسعة
10th	العاشر	العاشرة
11th	الحاديَ عَشَر	الحاديةَ عَشْرةَ
12th	الثاني عَشَر	الثانيةَ عَشْرةَ
13th	الثالثَ عشَر	الثالثةَ عَشْرةَ
14th	الرابعَ عشَر	الرابعةَ عَشْرةَ
15th	الخامسَ عشَر	الخامسةَ عَشْرةَ
16th	السادسَ عشَر	السادسةَ عَشْرةَ
17th	السابعَ عشَر	السابعةَ عَشْرةَ
18th	الثامنَ عشَر	الثامنةَ عَشْرةَ
19th	التاسعَ عشَر	التاسعةَ عَشْرةَ
20th	العشرون	العشرون
21st	الحادي والعشرونَ	الحادية والعشرونَ
22nd	الثاني والعشرونَ	الثانية والعشرونَ
23rd	الثالث والعشرونَ	الثالثة والعشرونَ

	Masculine	*Feminine*
30th	الثَلاثون	الثَلاثون
100th	المئة	المئة

2 Usage

Ordinal numbers are most commonly used as adjectives after nouns. They are usually found in the definite form, as shown in the table above.

Ordinal numbers follow the normal rules for adjectival agreement in terms of gender, number and case. However, as with the cardinal numbers, the numbers 11 to 19 do not vary:

الجبل الثالث	قنبلة سادسة
the third mountain	a sixth bomb
الشارع الحادي عَشَر	من الطالب الثالث والعشرين
the eleventh street	from the twenty-third student

Some ordinal numbers can also be used as superlative adjectives (*see* **Chapter 5, Section C**). For example, لأَوَّل مرّة is an alternative to للمرّة الأولى, meaning 'for the first time'.

C. FRACTIONS

'Half' is expressed as نِصْف in Arabic. The other fractions follow a common pattern similar to that of the ordinal numbers, as follows:

	Singular	*Plural*
half	نِصْف	
a third/thirds	ثُلْث	أَثْلاث
a quarter/quarters	رُبْع	أَرْباع
a fifth/fifths	خُمْس	أَخْماس
a sixth/sixths	سُدْس	أَسْداس
a seventh/sevenths	سُبْع	أَسْباع

an eighth/eighths	ثُمْن	أثْمان
a ninth/ninths	تُسْع	أتْساع
a tenth/tenths	عُشْر	أعْشار

These can be combined with cardinal numbers, or used in their dual form, to give compound fractions, for example:

ثلاثة أرْباع
three quarters

خمسة أثْمان
five eighths

ثلثان
two thirds *(dual form)*

 D. TIME AND DATES

The question 'what time is it?' can be expressed using كم الساعة؟ or
الساعة كم؟.

1 Full hours

In informal Arabic, full hours are formed using the cardinal numbers:

الساعة ستّة
it's six o'clock

For phrases such as 'at six o'clock', the ordinal number is used:

في الساعة الرابعة
at four o'clock

في الساعة الحادية عَشْرةَ
at eleven o'clock

2 Fractions of the hour

Fractions of the hour are expressed using نصْف (half), رُبْع
(quarter) and cardinal or ordinal numbers as appropriate:

الساعة الثانية والنصف
half past two

في الساعة الثالثة إلاّ خمس (دقائق)
at five (minutes) to three

في الساعة الثامنة وعشر (دقائق)
ten (minutes) past eight

3 Days of the week

Monday	(يَوْم) الاِثْنَيْن
Tuesday	(يَوْم) الثُّلاثاء
Wednesday	(يَوْم) الأَرْبعاء
Thursday	(يَوْم) الخَميس
Friday	(يَوْم) الجُمَعَة
Saturday	(يَوْم) السَّبْت
Sunday	(يَوْم) الأَحَد

4 Months

The names of the months vary from region to region. There are two main systems in use. The first forms given in the following table are used in Egypt and Sudan, while the forms shown in brackets are used in the area known as the Levant (Syria, Lebanon, Palestine and Jordan).

Some further variations exist in North Africa, where forms based on French pronunciation are in use. In addition, an Islamic system based on the lunar calendar is used for determining dates of religious significance such as the fasting month of مضان (Ramadan).

January	يَنَاير (كانُون الثَّاني)
February	فِبْرَاير (شُباط)
March	مَارِس (آذار)
April	إبْريل (نَيْسان)
May	مَايُو (أيَّار)
June	يُونِيه (حُزَيْران)
July	يُولِيه (تَمُوز)
August	أغُسْطِس (آب)
September	سِبْتَمْبِر (أيْلُول)

October	أُكْتُوبَر (تِشْرين الأوّل)
November	نُوفَمْبِر (تِشْرين الثّانِي)
December	دِيسَمْبِر (كانُون الأوّل)

5 Dates

Dates take the following form:

٢٣ يونيو ١٩٦٧

23 June 1967

In full, this would be read as:

الثّالِث والعِشْرون مِن (شَهر) يونيو سنةَ ألْف وتِسعمئة وسبع وستين

the twenty-third of June nineteen sixty-seven

17 SENTENCE STRUCTURE

A. NOMINAL SENTENCES

A nominal sentence is one which begins with either a subject noun or a pronoun.

Nominal sentences consist of two parts: the subject and the predicate. The subject is the person or thing that performs the action. The predicate provides information about the subject, and can be any type of word or phrase.

In the examples below, the predicate is underlined.

أحمد يدرس الطب في جامعة كسلا
Ahmed **studies medicine at Kassala University**

هي ذهبت إلى غزة في الصيف
she **went to Gaza in the summer**

The verb 'to be' is normally not used in the present tense. The most common nominal sentence consists of a definite subject followed by an indefinite noun or adjective or by a prepositional phrase. Both the subject and the predicate, where appropriate, take nominative case endings, but the verb 'to be' is not expressed:

البيتُ كبيرٌ	عليٌ مهندسٌ
(*lit.* the house big)	(*lit.* Ali an engineer)
the house **is big**	Ali **is an engineer**

الأستاذُ الجديدُ مغربيٌّ
the new teacher **is Moroccan**

هي طالبةٌ في قسم اللغة العربية
she **is a student in the Arabic department**

See also Chapter 13, Section J.

1 Nominal sentences with the 'sisters of إنَّ'

There is a special group of particles in Arabic known as the
'sisters of إنَّ'. These include:

indeed	إنَّ
that	أنَّ
as if	كأنَّ
but	لكنَّ
perhaps	لعلَّ
if only	لَيْت
because	لأنَّ

When these particles are followed by a nominal sentence, the
case endings in the sentence are affected. The predicate remains
nominative, but the subject becomes accusative:

| لعلّ القردَ مريضٌ | أحبّ الرياضة ولكنّ كرةَ القدم مملّةٌ |
| perhaps the monkey's sick | I like sport but football is boring |

إنَّ الطقسَ جميلٌ
indeed, the weather is beautiful

أعتقد أنَّ السائحينَ فرنسيّونَ
I think (that) the tourists are French

These particles may also have pronoun suffixes attached to them:

| لعلّه مريضٌ | أعتقد أنّهم فرنسيّونَ |
| perhaps he's sick | I think (that) they're French |

2 Nominal sentences with the 'sisters of كان'

There is a special group of verbs in Arabic known as the 'sisters
of كان'. These include:

to be	كان
not to be	ليس
to become	أصبح

to become	صار
to become	أمسى
to become	أضحى
to still be	ما زال
to still be	ظل
as long as	ما دام

When any form of these verbs is followed by a nominal sentence, the case endings in the sentence are affected. The subject remains nominative, but the predicate becomes accusative:

| ليس البيتُ كبيراً | كان الأستاذُ غنيّاً |
| the house isn't big | the teacher was rich |

ما زالت زينب مريضةً
Zeynab is still ill

في السنوات الأخيرة أصبحت الخرطوم مدينةً مزدحمةً
in recent years, Khartoum has become a crowded city

See also **Chapter 6** *for more on case endings.*

B. VERBAL SENTENCES

A verbal sentence is one which begins with a verb. The subject of the sentence may be expressed using a subject noun after the verb (explicit), or it may be indicated by the verb itself (implicit):

هرب السارق	هرب
the thief ran away	(*lit.* ran away)
	he ran away

When the subject of a verbal sentence is explicit, the subject always takes a nominative case ending.

In the following examples, the subject is underlined:

استمعت فوز إلى الراديو
Fouz listened to the radio

يريد مروان أن يهاجر إلى فرنسا
Marwan wants to emigrate to France

شاهدوا الفيلم الجديد في السينما
they watched the new film at the cinema

مساءً جلسنا في النادي حتى الساعة العاشرة
we sat in the club until 10pm

Note

A verbal sentence can have exactly the same meaning as a nominal sentence, but with different word order:

Nominal

عواطف تدرس اللغة التركية في الجامعة
Awatif studies Turkish at university

Verbal

تدرس عواطف اللغة التركية في الجامعة
Awatif studies Turkish at university

There is no significant difference in meaning between these two examples. While verbal sentences were the standard form in classical Arabic, modern Arabic is more flexible. In most contexts, however, verbal sentences are still considered better stylistically.

1 Verbal sentences with plural or dual subjects

When a verb appears at the start of a sentence it must be singular in number, even if the subject is a dual or plural noun. The verb agrees with the subject only in gender:

Nominal sentence	*Verbal sentence*
الطلاب يدرسون الاقتصاد	يدرس الطلاب الاقتصاد
the students study economics	the students study economics
ماجد وعمار سافرا إلى جيبوتي	سافر ماجد وعمار إلى جيبوتي
Majed and Ammar travelled to Djibouti	Majed and Ammar travelled to Djibouti

2 With an object

Some verbs require an object. The object can appear as a noun, or as a pronoun suffix attached to the verb. The object always takes an accusative case ending:

اشترت ندى فستاناً من السوق
Nada bought **a skirt** in the market

ضرب الولدُ الكلبَ
the boy hit **the dog**

زارنا سعيد في السنة الماضية
Saeed visited **us** last year

رأيناهم أول أمس
we saw **them** the day before yesterday

See also **Chapter 6** *for more on case endings.*

3 Object phrases

Arabic does not have a discrete category of words for adverbs. One way to describe an action in Arabic is to use an object phrase.

The construction 'verb + verbal noun' can be used either to describe or emphasize the verb's action, or to say how many times the action happened. The verbal noun acts like an object and takes an accusative case ending:

نمت نوماً عميقاً
(*lit.* I slept a deep sleep)
I slept deeply

ضرب الملاكم خصمه ضرباً شديداً
(*lit.* the boxer hit his opponent a hard hit)
the boxer hit his opponent hard

قرأت النص قراءتين
(*lit.* I read the text two readings)
I read the text twice

See also **Chapter 6, Section B.**

Object phrases can also be used to describe the reason for a
verb's action. However, in this case the verbal noun is not
formed from the same verb as the main action. Again, the verbal
noun acts like an object and takes an accusative case ending:

ضربت فاطمة أخاها كرهاً له
Fatima hit her brother because she hated him

أدرس اللغة العربية حبًا لها
I study Arabic because I love it

ذاكر أنس رغبةً في النجاح
Anas revised because he wanted to succeed

ساعدتُ العجوز شفقةً عليه
I helped the old man out of pity

C. EXCEPTION

1 With إلا

Arabic has a number of particles to express the English 'except'.
The most important of these is إلا:

نجح الطلاب إلا زيداً
the students passed, except for Zayd

The noun that follows the particle إلا must be accusative if both
the general noun (eg 'the **students** passed') and the excepted
noun (eg 'except for **Zayd**') are mentioned in the sentence:

أحب الفواكه إلا البرتقالَ

I like fruit, except for oranges

If both the general noun and the excepted noun are mentioned in a sentence negated by ما, the excepted noun can be either accusative or can be marked for case according to its position in the sentence:

ما أكلت فواكه إلا تفاحًا

I didn't eat fruit, except for apples

ما جاء ضيوف إلا جميلٌ/جميلًا

no guests came, except Jamil

ما لعبت مع زملاء إلا مع زاهدٍ/زاهدًا

I didn't play with friends, except for Zahid

If the general noun is not mentioned in the sentence, the excepted noun is marked for case according to its position in the sentence:

ما نجح إلا زيدٌ

(*lit.* no-one succeeded except Zayd)

only Zayd succeeded

ما قابلت إلا زيداً

(*lit.* I didn't meet anyone except Zayd)

I only met Zayd

ما لعبت إلا مع زيد

I only played with Zayd

2 With غير

Another particle used to express exception is غير. This noun is used as the first term in a genitive construction and the excepted noun that follows it must be in the genitive case:

ما حضرُ غيرُ طالب
(*lit.* no-one came other than a student)
only a student came

ما رأيت غيرَ طالب
I only saw a student

3 With خلا, عدا and حاشا

Other constructions that express exception include خلا, عدا and حاشا, which can be used either as verbs or as prepositions. The excepted noun that follows must be in the accusative or genitive case:

حضر الجميع عدا المديرَ/المديرِ
everyone came except the director

حفظت الكلمات الجديدة عدا واحدةً/واحدةٍ
I learned all the new words except one

When used in combination with ما, the excepted noun is accusative:

حضر الجميع ما عدا المديرَ
everyone came except the director

حفظت الكلمات الجديدة ما عدا واحدةً
I learned all the new words except one

D. WONDER AND EXCLAMATION

There are two ways to express wonder and exclamation in Arabic, using ما أَفْعَل and أَفْعِل به. These expressions appear to be based on superlative adjectives, but are in fact Form IV verbs (*see* **Chapter 13, Section G**). As such they are followed either by a noun in the accusative or by a pronoun suffix. In modern Arabic, the first type of expression is the more common.

ما أوسع المكتب!
how spacious the office is!

ما أجمل الموسيقى!
how beautiful the music is!

أكرم بحسن!
how generous Hasan is!

أحسن بالطالب المجتهد!
how good the hardworking student is!

Verbs used in this kind of sentence are not marked for gender and number:

ما أكرم الأستاذ!
how generous the teacher is! *(m)*

أكرم بالأستاذ/أكرم به
how generous the teacher is! *(m)*

ما أكرم الأستاذة!
how generous the teacher is! *(f)*

أكرم بالأستاذة/أكرم بها
how generous the teacher is! *(f)*

ما أكرم الأساتذة!
how generous the teachers are!

أكرم بالأساتذة/أكرم بهم
how generous the teachers are!

E. PRAISE AND BLAME

Praise is expressed in Arabic by the verb نِعْمَ and blame by the verb بِئْسَ. Although these verbs are formed using the perfect (past) tense, their meaning is imperfect (present). They do not change according to the number or gender of their subject:

نِعْمَ المعلِّمُ محمدٌ!
how good the teacher Muhammad is!

نِعْمَ المعلّمةُ ناديةٌ!
how good the teacher Nadia is!

بِئْسَ الطالبةُ ماجدةٌ!
how bad the student Majida is!

بِئْسَ الطالبُ ماجدٌ!
how bad the student Majid is!

Another way of expressing praise is by using the verb حبّذا. Blame can also be expressed using the verb لا حبّذا:

حبّذا صادقاً زيدٌ!
how truthful Zayd is!

لا حبّذا كاذباً ماجدٌ!
what a liar Majid is!

حبّذا الصدق!
how good truthfulness is!

لا حبّذا الكذب!
how horrid lying is!

F. CONDITIONAL SENTENCES

A conditional sentence consists of two parts, or clauses. One clause gives the condition (eg 'if I were to win the lottery'), and the other gives the result of the condition (eg 'I'd buy a house'). There are several particles used to express condition in Arabic, including لو, إن and إذا.

1 With لو

Hypothetical and unlikely conditions are expressed using لو. The condition clause and the result clause follow this particle and are usually in the perfect tense. The result clause is generally introduced by the particle ل.

Note that the meaning of the conditional sentence can be either past or present tense:

لو كنتُ الأستاذ، لأعطيت الطلاب واجبات أقل
if I were the teacher, I'd give the students less homework/if I'd been the teacher, I would've given the students less homework

لو كان عندي المبلغ الذي تحتاجه، لأعطيتك إياه
if I had the sum you need, I'd give it to you/if I'd had the sum you needed, I'd have given it to you

لو كنت أستطيع السباحة، لأنقذتها من الغرق
if I could swim, I would save her from drowning/if I could swim, I would've saved her from drowning

2 With إذا and إن

Other types of condition are expressed using the particles إذا

and إنْ. The condition clause that follows the particle is either in the perfect tense or the jussive, the perfect being more common in modern Arabic. The result clause can be either perfect or imperfect. If the result clause is imperfect, it is usually introduced by ف, particularly if it is future in meaning or expresses an order:

إذا سافر أخي إلى لبنان، سافرت معه	إن سافر أخي إلى لبنان، فأسافر معه
if my brother travels to Lebanon, I'll travel with him	if my brother travels to Lebanon, I'll travel with him
إذا أسافر إلى لبنان، تسافر معي	إن أسافر إلى لبنان، سافرت معي
if I travel to Lebanon, you'll travel with me	if I travel to Lebanon, you'll travel with me
إذا سافرت إلى لبنان، فستسافر معي	إن سافرتَ إلى لبنان، فخذني معك
if you travel to Lebanon, you'll travel with me	if you travel to Lebanon, take me with you

See **Chapter 13, Sections B** *and* C.

3 With other particles

Other particles that express condition include متى, اينما, من, ما, and كيفما.

These particles can be followed by a condition clause in either the perfect or jussive tense. The verb in the result clause will also be in the jussive:

من يجتهدْ ينجحْ
he who makes an effort will succeed

ما تزرعْ اليوم تحصدْ غدا
what you sow today, you will harvest tomorrow

أينما تسافر، فستجدنا معك
wherever you travel, you will find us with you

مهما تبتعد، فسنظل صديقين
however far away you are, we will stay friends

G. THE VOCATIVE

The vocative is used to call someone or to attract someone's attention. The most important vocative particle is يا. This particle must be followed by a noun that refers to the person being called. If the noun that follows the particle is a proper noun or if it is definite but not part of an idāfa construction, then it will be nominative:

يا ماجدٌ، اسمعني!
Majid, listen to me!

يا جميلةُ، أسرعي!
Jamila, hurry up!

See **Chapter 4** *for more on noun forms.*

If the noun that follows the vocative particle is indefinite, it becomes accusative:

يا نائماً، انتبه!
pay attention, you sleepy man!

يا كسولاً، اعمل!
work, you lazybones!

If the noun that follows the vocative particle is part of an idāfa construction, it becomes accusative:

يا بنَ عمي، ساعدني!
help me, cousin!

يا فاعل الخير، أبشر!
rejoice, doer of good!

يا طلابَ الجامعة، احضروا جميع الدروس!
university students, attend all classes!

INDEX